Event
Success

Alon Alroy — Eran Ben-Shushan — Boaz Katz

Event Success

Maximizing the Business
Impact of In-person, Virtual,
and Hybrid Experiences

WILEY

For general information on our other products and services or for technical support, please contact our Customer Care Department within the United States at (800) 762-2974, outside the United States at (317) 572-3993 or fax (317) 572-4002.

Wiley publishes in a variety of print and electronic formats and by print-on-demand. Some material included with standard print versions of this book may not be included in e-books or in print-on-demand. If this book refers to media such as a CD or DVD that is not included in the version you purchased, you may download this material at http://booksupport.wiley.com. For more information about Wiley products, visit www.wiley.com.

Library of Congress Cataloging-in-Publication Data

Names: Alroy, Alon, author. | Ben-Shushan, Eran, author. | Katz, Boaz, author.
Title: Event success : maximizing the business impact of in-person, virtual, and hybrid experiences / Alon Alroy, Eran Ben-Shushan, and Boaz Katz.
Description: Hoboken, New Jersey : Wiley, [2022] | Includes bibliographical references and index.
Identifiers: LCCN 2021059918 (print) | LCCN 2021059919 (ebook) | ISBN 9781119817154 (cloth) | ISBN 9781119817208 (adobe pdf) | ISBN 9781119817161 (epub)
Subjects: LCSH: Special events. | Marketing.
Classification: LCC GT3405 .A57 2022 (print) | LCC GT3405 (ebook) | DDC 394.2—dc23/eng/20220105
LC record available at https://lccn.loc.gov/2021059918
LC ebook record available at https://lccn.loc.gov/2021059919

Cover Design: Bizzabo
Cover Image: © Bizzabo

SKY10032491_020422

*To our dearest families, to Bizzaboers around the world,
and to the event experience leaders who bring us all together*

Contents

Part I   Why Events?   1

Chapter 1   How We Got Here   3

Chapter 2   Event Success in the Post-COVID-19 Era   15

Chapter 3   After the Storm   25

Part II   Data   35

Chapter 4   The Age of Disruption   37

Chapter 5   The Event Data Maturity Curve   45

Chapter 6   Reaching the Right Audience at the Right Time   51

Chapter 7   SAPPHIRE NOW: A Case Study in Event Data Utilization   61

Chapter 8   With New Data Power Comes New Responsibility   71

Part III   Audience Engagement   **77**

Chapter 9   Engagement in a Hybrid Era   79

Chapter 10   Choosing the Right Format for the
                 Right Outcome   91

Chapter 11   Content   103

Chapter 12   Community   115

Chapter 13   Experience Design   125

Part IV   People and Process   **135**

Chapter 14   The Rise of the Event Experience Manager 137

Chapter 15   New Skills for a New Title   147

Chapter 16   Soft Skills   157

Chapter 17   The New Path for Event Professionals 169

Chapter 18   The Event Team of the Future   177

Part V   Technology   **187**

Chapter 19   The Changing Event Technology
                 Landscape   189

Chapter 20   Choosing the Right Technology Partner 197

Chapter 21   What an Event Platform Can (and Can't)
                 Do for You   221

Chapter 22   Taking on the Future of Experiences   227

Contents

References 237

Acknowledgments 241

About Bizzabo 245

About the Authors 247

Index 251

PART

Why Events?

1

How We Got Here

Live events shape history.

Pick any moment in time—the Industrial Revolution, the Enlightenment, the Roman Forum, the biblical era—and you'll find a congregation of people and the sharing of ideas to be the definitive force of progress and innovation of the age.

Gathering to debate and share ideas is such a natural human tendency that it was rare to find people who questioned the value of this practice. Some might prefer certain events over others, some might attend out of necessity rather than interest, but the value of attending events—of being at the center of those ideas and debates and decisions—was rarely called into question. At least until very recently.

Back in 2019, we published a collection of quotes from conversations with event leaders. These quotes were pulled from our IN-PERSON podcast series, where we feature the world's most daring events and the people who make them happen. The book ranged from topics like experiences to community to team leadership, but one of the first topics we covered was the most inspiring: "Why events?"[1] The answers, as you might expect, ran the gamut but shared a common theme. Here are a few of the quoted answers:

Chardia Christophe-Garcia, then a marketing director at Forbes: "More and more we're seeing that the event landscape

---

[1] The actual title of the chapter was "Why In-Person," a decision intended to reflect our IN-PERSON content brand and our steadfast belief in the power of in-person experiences. Admittedly, the prospect of virtual events becoming so popular and necessary was very far away at the time.

isn't going anywhere. People want experiences. They want to have that one-to-one connection and networking."

Lindsay Niemic McKenna, then vice president of revenue marketing at Yext: "People understand that human connection is really important, especially as we're becoming a more digitized world."

Hugh Forrest, chief programming officer at SXSW: As much as we've changed and improved technology to be able to connect with people, nothing yet replaces real-time, face-to-face interactions in terms of creating new opportunities."

Colleen Bisconti, vice president of global conferences and events at IBM: "We're seeing that the events are still the primary driver of marketing results. Events touch almost every single opportunity that progresses and ultimately closes. So it's a great place to be, and it's a great way to lean in and to provide business results. And that's why I love it so much."

An event, at its core, is about community building: gathering people around a shared idea, vision, goal, market vertical, or story. In the modern context, and specifically in relation to corporate events, it's an opportunity to share the brand's story, to turn a slogan or a product or an idea into a tangible experience. It's an opportunity for businesses, nonprofits, and for-profit event organizers to show the world who they are and what they stand for during an intense (but limited) time frame. It's the one big chance many get each year to deliver an important message to a captive audience. It's an opportunity to celebrate and showcase a brand's achievements.

Events are also a key opportunity to grow business. In marketing terms, events offer value at virtually every stage of the sales funnel, from awareness to conversion and everything in between. They are a venue for finding new business, upselling old business, or simply strengthening relationships with customers and partners in hopes of improving future business. If you want to drive sales, history has proven that events are a great way to do so.

Finally, events are key to strengthening internal relationships. Just as they can facilitate commerce, they can also facilitate camaraderie. Business is based on relationships, and throughout history humanity has relied on shared experiences to establish or strengthen those bonds. Events are where those "hallway moments" happen—when relationships built on financial incentives, convenience, or coincidence evolve into something more concrete.

In short, events just kind of work, and always have. As long as they evolve.

Overcoming a History of Inertia

Events are such natural value creators that the industry behind live events has long faced a strong resistance to change. After all, events often accomplished the desired outcome for those who were organizing them, at least to the extent that they could measure that success, so who would take a costly gamble on change?

Furthermore, many organizations operate around a single annual flagship event, which would be the last place they wanted to experiment. You know the feeling of being on your toes, putting out metaphorical (or perhaps in some cases, literal) fires as they arise. In this high-stress environment, the safe option is often preferred, even at the cost of innovation. We can't blame anyone who's trying to facilitate an experience for 100, 1,000, 10,000, or 100,000 people for being risk averse, for falling back on tried-and-true methods and processes, for taking the route that gives them one less thing to worry about in the midst of their big event.

The other reason for such strong inertia in the events industry was that experimentation was also risky on an individual level. If your higher-ups think last year's event went well, why risk drastic changes that could threaten your career? Event organizing can be a thankless job. Having your event run smoothly is a baseline expectation. Sure, there are minor problems that can be improved on from year to year, but most changes go unnoticed—unless they cause a problem. Why risk your career to advocate for change when nobody is calling for it?

Obviously, this is a broad characterization. There are plenty of exceptions, many of which we will highlight in these very pages. Countless event heroes out there shook things up, pushed the needle, and took chances, and we wholeheartedly celebrate their boldness.

But while most industries were adopting an evolve-or-die mentality in the early 2000s and into the 2010s as a result of rapid technological innovation, the events industry found itself naturally inclined to take the opposite route. Rather than feeling pressured to evolve, as so many industries did during that time, event organizers were often under pressure to repeat last year's success—which was based on the year prior, which was based on the year before that, and so on.

According to industry thought leader Marco Giberti, "The formula works well, and it's successful, and it's growing, and it's sustainable in many ways." He told us recently over Zoom, "Most organizers—corporate, for profit, or associations—were using a playbook that was solid and successful, growing nicely, and the overall reaction was, 'Why should I change if this is working?' There's no urgency for deep innovation, there's no urgency for transformation, because it's going pretty well."

That old playbook, however, has since been rendered obsolete. For the first time, event organizers are now finding themselves in completely uncharted territory and are now being challenged to reinvent an industry long resistant to change.

An Industry Ripe for Disruption

On the surface it appeared that the events industry had been growing steadily; budgets were increasing, attendee numbers were growing, and event organizers were being given license to curate incredible experiences for their audiences.

Apple, IBM, Microsoft, Cisco, Google, Salesforce, Amazon—nearly every major technology company produced a major flagship event for tens of thousands of attendees. Meanwhile, staging a flagship conference became a mark of success for thousands of emerging technology companies. And all this is to say nothing about how nonprofits, associations, media companies, and financial institutions leverage events to drive their own business goals.

A 2018 report published by the Events Industry Council reported that, accounting for indirect and induced impacts, events supported a global economic impact of $2.5 trillion of business sales, 26 million jobs, and $1.5 trillion of GDP. According to a 2021 report from Allide Marketing, the events industry was valued at $1,135.4 billion in 2019 and is expected to reach $1,552.9 billion by 2028, registering a compound annual growth rate of 11.2 percent from 2021 to 2028.[2]

Below the surface, however, Marco Giberti says events were simultaneously experiencing a gradual decline—so gradual that it largely went unnoticed. In recent years, the **Net Promoter**

---

[2]https://dev-meetingsmeanbusiness.pantheonsite.io/sites/default/files/OE-EIC%20
Global%20Meetings%20Significance%20(FINAL)%202018-11-09-2018.pdf.

Score (NPS)—a metric used to measure customer loyalty—was flat at best. It was not a dramatic trend by any means, but it suggested something worth considering: both exhibitors and attendees weren't excited about the events they were going to. In other words, the experience of events was missing the mark.

What prevented many decision makers from seeing this decline involved the reliance on business models and benchmarks. The real estate model, for example, more often than not dictated the financial structure of some events. These events were often approached as a simple math equation: X square feet of exhibition space, divided by Y exhibitors, times $Z per square foot in the receivable column; marketing budgets, speaker fees, venue rental, catering costs, and other expenses in the payable column. So long as the revenue generated exceeded expenses, the event was in the black and was considered a success. If certain exhibitors or attendees had a negative experience, it didn't really matter as long as space (and registrations) sold out the following year.

In cases where profitability from exhibitors, sponsors, and registration sales was not the desired outcome (as for many corporate events), event organizers lacked a common set of benchmarks for evaluating how an event contributed to key business outcomes.

Proving event success, or **return on events (ROE)** as we call it, has long been an incomplete science with event organizers measuring the performance of events on a simple basis—if at all—without a clear understanding of the impact an event has on business outcomes. There was always a sense that things were working as intended, even if "how" or "why" couldn't be precisely measured or explained. The lack of quality metrics to measure vital benchmarks like attendee experience, exhibitor and attendee return on investment, the overall quality of the experience, and so on, created a blind spot for the industry, and in that blind spot complacence was growing.

Unlike most industries at the turn of the millennium, live events had no external forces pressuring them to evolve, no new source of disruption, no real risk of being left behind in the digital era. The only risk was innovating too much too quickly, and inadvertently putting a wrench in an otherwise well-oiled machine.

A Temporary Pause and a Permanent Change

In March 2020, as the COVID-19 pandemic began sweeping across the globe, we watched our internal dashboards as major sponsors started pulling out of events and organizers began postponing and eventually canceling their flagship conferences.

In the ensuing months we heard stories from partners, colleagues, customers, and friends about the internal turmoil that was playing out in event teams around the world. The economic uncertainty of the moment, coupled with the restrictions put in place to limit the spread of the virus, resulted in event budgets getting slashed, team members getting laid off, and widespread uncertainty about the future of events.

Up until that moment, the live events industry felt untouchable. Suddenly, it felt like a hurricane was barreling toward us, and there was nothing we could do but board up the windows and hope for the best.

It was an incredibly painful time for us personally, for our growing events technology platform, and for the industry at large. We, like many others in the industry, had to cut our team by 25 percent, knowing that in the coming months we would either be in a position to hire them back or not have a company at all.

After decades of inertia, the industry was forced to adopt the innovation it had long resisted and seek to reinvent itself. Experimentation and innovation were suddenly no longer a matter of choice, but of survival. As we emerge on the other end of the pandemic, one thing is for sure: the events industry will never be the same. In the coming years, the very definition of the word *events* will change dramatically, as will the way we measure ROE and event success in the post-COVID-19 era.

A New Day Has Dawned

Since those dark early days of the pandemic, we've watched as an industry pushed to the brink quickly adopted the necessary tools, skills, and capabilities required to completely reinvent itself in an impossibly short time frame. What could have ultimately spelled the end of events as we knew it instead proved to be the push the industry had long needed to reach its full potential in the Digital Age.

We are only at the starting point of a whole new events industry, and the playbook is still being written, but already we see three key themes that will improve success in the future of events: management, engagement, and growth.

Management

We steadfastly believe that the future of events is about experience-first design—that is, overcoming the decline in NPS scores by creating events that take into consideration the entire suite of stakeholder experiences—from when they first visit a website to the way that they connect with other stakeholders to navigation of the event itself. In order to make this vision a reality, event managers—or **event experience managers**, as we refer to them—will need to continue to revisit the ways that they manage their strategies and their processes for working with their teams to arrive at these strategies. In order to overcome the challenges of this new chapter in event history, the event team itself will have to undergo a significant transformation.

Moving forward, event professionals will need to demonstrate a variety of new skills, ranging from hard technical skills to softer skills like empathy and collaboration, while working across multidisciplinary teams. The makeup of the team itself will also need to evolve in order to overcome new challenges, adding new types of expertise that weren't as necessary previously, while reforming some roles that have become obsolete.

Part of this transition will be revisiting and redefining how event teams interact with other teams within their organization.

Engagement

Engagement is a key attribute of a successful event, but the way in which organizers reach audiences and design experiences for them is undergoing a dramatic transformation. Gone are the days of a captive audience that dedicates multiple days to in-person event attendance by default.

Moving forward, organizers are going to have to get creative in order to pique the interest of an audience that is always one click away from the exit. Event teams are now being challenged by the need to engage audiences that are less likely to attend as many events in person and less likely to dedicate as much time to their events. Key to achieving strong ROE is cracking the code on event engagement in these new formats.

Growth

We live in a world where everything can be measured, especially if it takes place in a virtual setting. With new virtual platforms, events are becoming powerful data generators, and the utilization of this data is key to event success. Furthermore, event success and ROI have long been tied to quantitative metrics like attendee and registration numbers, or square footage of exhibition space, rather than qualitative metrics, like engagement, lead generation, and brand affinity. In most other industries, such metrics are seen as vital benchmarks and tools for optimization, for understanding the audiences' needs and habits, and for improving the quality of the product.

As we emerge from the pandemic into an age of virtual and hybrid events, data will begin to play a much bigger role in measuring, optimizing, and ultimately scaling event success. To some, these changes might sound intimidating, but we encourage everyone in the industry to see this evolution for what it is: an opportunity for events to become more purposeful, more impactful, more demonstrably valuable, and more efficient in achieving their stated aims. Though the disruption of the pandemic was a shock to event professionals, we will (and are already beginning to) look back at that moment as a key enabler of innovation in an industry that was in desperate need of change.

2

Event Success in the Post-COVID-19 Era

The pandemic has changed our very definition of events, and with it comes a new definition of event success. Prior to COVID-19, virtual events were few and far between. They also often failed to offer much of what inspired people to attend events in person. Such events (webinars, webcasts, online conferences, and digital trade shows) were often effective in achieving specific outcomes, but they were hardly considered a viable alternative to the in-person experience.

As the pandemic progressed, however, the industry as a whole made some incredible strides in improving the virtual event experience—progress that will continue well after in-person events resume. Throughout the remainder of 2020 and the first half of 2021, we saw incredible levels of resilience, adaptability, technological adoption, and rapid innovation. While the sudden transition to virtual events posed a lot of challenges, it also offered a range of new opportunities.

Challenges and Opportunities Associated with Virtual Events

According to a study we conducted in 2020, 68 percent of event marketers believe it is more difficult to facilitate networking opportunities when hosting virtual events, 67.7 percent struggled to maintain engagement, and 52.5 percent were challenged by the logistics of virtual events.

Up until this point, our entire industry was built around face-to-face human interaction, whether on stage, on the exhibition floor, or after hours. Organizers faced the immediate challenge of replicating those interactions, and many are still struggling to overcome this. Keeping virtual audiences engaged, especially during a pandemic that forced many to work from home, was especially daunting. Event organizers have long enjoyed the benefits of a captive audience, but suddenly found themselves competing with everything from incoming emails and phone calls to a dog barking or baby crying in the background. Furthermore, event teams are experts at facilitating in-person experiences, from booking venues to managing logistics, but producing a virtual experience often requires different skills and different tools. Despite these challenges, however, both virtual and hybrid events (which contain elements of both in-person and virtual experiences) offer a range of benefits.

According to our research, 60 percent of event professionals pivoted an in-person event to a virtual format as a direct result of the pandemic in 2020. That year, 80 percent of event organizers said they were able to reach a wider audience with virtual events, more than half increased the number of webinars they produced, and 71.5 percent say virtual engagement tools will play a major role in their event strategies moving forward. In fact, 65.5 percent said their budgets will increase, and 93 percent plan to invest in virtual events in the future.

Virtual events are relatively less expensive to produce than their in-person counterparts, and the shift to a virtual format will dramatically increase their reach. They are also powerful data generators, providing valuable insights on attendee engagement patterns, potentially offering clues to buying behaviors.

An Early Case Study

We at Bizzabo got a first-hand look at both the opportunities and the challenges associated with virtual events at a relatively early stage in the pandemic, and our experience was not unlike others in the events space.

Prior to the pandemic we had hosted a few events of our own—including our IN-PERSON Collective flagship event that took place in New York in December 2019—but the majority of our understanding of events was informed by conversations with our customers and partners in the industry.

As we pivoted toward becoming a virtual events platform in early 2020, we decided to put our new virtual event platform to the test by hosting our own virtual event, which we called (Almost) IN-PERSON.

We sent out invitations to members of the industry in hopes of attracting 500 attendees. Within 24 hours, we had 1,500 registrants. After 72 hours, we reached 5,000. In the end, we had more than 6,000 participants across 70 countries, including representatives from companies like Twitter, Salesforce, and Amazon—the types of brands whose business we had been chasing for years (unsuccessfully, up to that point).

We also received responses from current and prospective investors and most of our biggest clients. We had to figure out a lot for the first time in a very condensed time frame, such as whether virtual events also needed an app (they do) and whether the event should be broadcast live or should rely on prerecorded videos (we did both and learned that attendees definitely appreciate knowing whether or not a session is actually happening live). We experienced a wide array of technical glitches in the days and weeks leading up to the event, as we scrambled to cobble together a viable virtual events platform, but when the moment came, everything went off without a hitch.

It was an incredibly powerful moment for us as individuals, as a company, but above all, as an industry. In the previous few weeks we had all experienced layoffs, budget cuts, uncertainty about the future—nobody in the industry was immune. We had no choice but to build our way out of it, and from that effort we had the opportunity to show everyone that there really *was* a viable complement to in-person events, that events still had relevance during COVID-19, and that we all still had a future in this industry.

We wanted to bring the industry together not just to commiserate on how unfortunate we all were to be in the middle of this storm, but to shift the narrative and demonstrate how this was actually an opportunity to implement some much-needed change. We had gone from being one of the hardest-hit industries in one of the hardest periods of human history to flipping the script and seizing a once-in-a-lifetime opportunity to move events toward a better future.

(Almost) IN-PERSON proved to be a turning point for our company, and dare we say the industry at large. Up until that point we felt like we were stuck playing defense, but after just a few short weeks we were now on the offensive. By the end of the year, we had gone from cutting our staff by a quarter to nearly doubling its original size. In December, we closed a $138 million financing round, our largest to date.

A Chorus of Aha Moments

We were an early adopter of a model that proved successful not only for ourselves, but for other major players in the live events space in the weeks and months to come. At the start of the pandemic we thought the future of our company was in jeopardy, but somewhere along the line, in the lead-up to (Almost) IN-PERSON, we experienced an "aha" moment, when all the challenges suddenly felt small, and the opportunity felt immense. As it turns out, we were far from alone in experiencing that sudden transition from a feeling of desperation to a feeling of possibility.

When the pandemic began, Colleen Bisconti was only eight weeks away from producing IBM's largest annual event, Think.

Despite the sudden disruption, it was decided that the event would move forward as scheduled, but on a virtual platform. Colleen says she immediately faced a range of challenges, from technical to operational to practical, as she and her team quickly adopted a completely foreign venue format.

In order to redesign Think in a virtual format, she began by deconstructing the event. She identified the reasons people attended in the past, focusing her efforts on delivering that value in a virtual format.

"What we found was that we had way bigger reach; we had over 100,000 people actually register for this, because it was free and available to anyone, anywhere," she says. "What that taught us was that we could extend our reach way broader than ever before, and it allowed us to reach more clients and prospective clients, more people within the accounts of our key clients."

On the other side of the pond, Orson Francescone was facing the reality of cancelling the Financial Times (FT) Live's 200 annual global events, which typically included a small in-person crowd of a few hundred each. At the start of the pandemic, FT Live decided to host a three-day virtual event called "The Global Boardroom," bringing together some of the world's top economists, business leaders, and lawmakers to break down the financial implications of the pandemic.

"We entered day one of the Global Boardroom with 25,000 registrations; by the end of day three we had 52,000 registrations, so basically 25,000 people registered throughout the event as the word spread," he says. "Consumer behaviors were very different: I can register at the last minute, I don't need to book a plane ticket, I don't need to book a hotel, I don't need to book time off, so I'll decide 20 minutes before if I want to join or not join. That was kind of mind blowing. The fact that our registrations doubled during the event was pretty incredible."

What Colleen and Orson discovered was that even with limited resources and a condensed time frame, they could still deliver value to a broad virtual audience. After that experience, neither intended to revert to an in-person-by-default mentality, even after it was safe to do so.

And they were not alone.

Digital by Default

As Orson and Colleen discovered early on in the pandemic, and as we did ourselves, virtual events dramatically increase a brand's reach. The initial excitement over registration and attendee numbers, however, was a vestige of the industry's past; event teams have long been accustomed to measuring success in terms of registrations and attendees. As the pandemic progressed and organizers got more sophisticated in their virtual event strategies, they discovered an ability to gather even more telling metrics, and began reconsidering how to benchmark an event's success.

Having a bigger audience is nice, but what really matters is how you engage with that audience—and by extension, how your audience engages with you. That's where data comes in. As events shift to a hybrid platform (where both in-person and virtual experiences are on the table) it becomes easier to track the attendee journey and cater experiences specifically to their needs.

This new approach to event success, ironically, has made it difficult for organizers to see themselves reverting back to an entirely in-person strategy in the future. The data that's generated from hybrid event platforms is so powerful, and the extended reach of virtual events so appealing, that the online format has quickly gone from a last resort to the first.

"What we wanted to do was take advantage of this blank slate that we had and say, 'When events come back, we really need to think differently about the way that they come back,' because we knew that the landscape would be permanently disrupted," explained Nicola Kastner, the vice president and global head of event strategy at SAP. "What we did was take a data-driven approach to formulating our overall event strategy."

Nicola tells us that in considering the future of events, she and her team studied four specific areas: attendee needs, SAP's marketing strategy, how to define event success, and how other industries had reacted to similar disruptions. Through that exercise, her team identified several findings that matched opportunities and trends raised by many event professionals across the industry, from how virtual attendee behaviors differ from in-person attendee behaviors to a trend toward smaller, local events over major international ones.

"All of these things have formulated our approach, so I believe we will take a much more localized, targeted approach to how we build our events in the future," she says.

Nicola isn't the only one rethinking the effectiveness of the massive, in-person, flagship event that has long been the centerpiece of many organizations' event strategy.

"We will go back to live events, but we will go back only if and when it makes sense, both from our point of view and our clients' point of view," says Orson of FT Live's new event strategy. "We don't want to lose hold of those new engaged global audiences, and the only way to do that is to maintain a digital-first approach to our events, even when we go back to physical [events]."

"We're going to be digital first, and physical with purpose," adds Colleen, describing IBM's new event strategy. "This is a chance for us to reinvent how we think about face-to-face interactions, and where we show up, and how we show up. I think it would be a missed opportunity if any of us jumped back to the old ways of thinking."

CHAPTER

3

After the Storm

COVID-19 marked a permanent shift in the events industry—one many felt was badly needed—and we are humbled and motivated by the opportunity to play a role in its evolution.

Ever since we founded Bizzabo, in the dawn of the age of mobile technology, just about every industry around us has gone through a significant transformation. When the company was founded, we were still phoning taxi dispatchers, renting movies from a store, buying (or burning) CDs, and doing most, if not all, of our shopping in person with cash.

Much about our world is dramatically different now, but until recently the events industry remained largely the same. Previously, the industry had no external pressure to evolve, facing no outside threats to its supremacy, with no reason to believe change was safer than the status quo. Unlike other industries, disruption would have likely never come in the form of a smaller, nimbler, well-funded start-up, and the industry could have continued on gently tiptoeing toward progress at a safe speed for the foreseeable future.

Instead, our disruptor came in the form of a global pandemic, and now events will be rushing toward the kind of innovations that will make the industry more resilient, more sustainable, and more impactful moving forward.

The Event Impact Gap™

Event professionals now have a mandate to create immersive, personalized hybrid experiences, combining their deep knowledge of in-person event strategy with the opportunities presented by digital tools and capabilities. Unfortunately, many still struggle to deliver on that mandate.

The challenges that organizers face can be summed up in what we call the **Event Impact Gap™**: the enormous chasm between the aspiration that event organizers have to create immersive, connected, and personalized human experiences and their ability to deliver them with their current technology, skills, and processes. From our own experiences and from speaking to hundreds of event professionals, we've determined that four major problems have caused the Event Impact Gap™:

1. **Data:** Customer and event data are either missing or captured in isolation, so it's hard to see and measure progress toward business outcomes.

2. **Audience Engagement:** Event leaders do not have the tools or frameworks to truly connect with audiences. As a result, audiences remain siloed and not truly present.

3. **People and Process:** Event professionals find it challenging to stay up to date with the operating know-how and the concierge-level service needed in this evolving event landscape.

4. **Technology:** The available tools are neither intuitive nor truly flexible, preventing event leaders from being able to design unique experiences in a hybrid world.

These critical problems have only been underscored by the opportunities and challenges of the hybrid era where brands, enterprises, and nonprofits depend on event professionals to create personalized, multichannel experiences that deliver measurable results, regardless of the attendees' location.

Throughout this book, we will review ideas, advice, and examples around these four problems of the Event Impact Gap™.

Data

Data has the potential to capture, connect, and leverage event leaders' most valuable customer and experience data, but many event professionals still struggle to effectively utilize their data. Doing so, however, becomes even more important in a virtual environment, where data is more readily available.

Data has impacted nearly every industry in a dramatic way (and arguably none more than digital marketing), yet live events seemed relatively immune to the data revolution—at least until now. As technology becomes a bigger piece of the live events puzzle, data will turn ROE from a gut feeling into a precise measurement, and that measurement will help the industry articulate its value in precise terms.

Rexson Serrao, the senior director of marketing technology (brand and events) for Salesforce, explains that he, like many others in the industry, had gotten accustomed to repeating the previous year's success and had not really taken a hard look at the company's data assets. It wasn't until the disruption of the pandemic that he began to question conventional wisdom, specifically as it concerned data.

"One of the most important takeaways is, go back to the first principles, go back to the why, get back to the basics, and look at the data in a whole new way, not just reporting on stats, but looking at some of those insights," he said, on an episode of the IN-PERSON podcast published back in June 2021. "You start to challenge the data a little bit and start to ask, 'I get what the statistic is, but what did it actually drive?'"

"One virtual event was able to generate, just in terms of raw count, more data points than the entirety of our in-person portfolio last year," Rexson explains. "Trying to make sense of that really was the biggest challenge."

Data has the potential to inform internal decision making, improve audience experiences, and ultimately drive ROE. Doing so will require the collection and utilization of basic metrics like conversion rates and speaker performance; engagement metrics like networking effectiveness and satisfaction scores; and growth results like pipeline acceleration, communication engagement, and sponsor ROI.

Realizing the full potential of this trove of data remains a significant barrier to closing the Event Impact Gap™, and one we will explore further in Part 2 with the help of a variety of industry leaders.

Audience Engagement

Moving forward, audiences are going to have far greater access to far more events through virtual and hybrid event formats. As seen during the pandemic, however, attendees will also have the option to attend only the one or two sessions that are specifically relevant to them, rather than commit to a full day's (or multiple days') worth of scheduled programming. As a result, organizers will seek to deliver highly targeted and highly relevant content that has real value to a niche audience. That is a far cry from the event programming of the past.

Combining the availability of data and the need to deliver real value to attendees will eventually lead to a highly personalized event experience. Rather than delivering the same message to 15,000 guests, events will increasingly offer those same attendees 15,000 unique experiences based on their specific needs. Artificial intelligence tools are already improving the way in which prospective attendees discover relevant content, speakers, and networking opportunities.

Moving forward, we envision the industry adopting a model similar to content streaming platforms, where attendees are recommended content based on their interests and previous habits. Rather than spending hours digging through agendas to find the handful of presentations that offer real substantive value, organizers will utilize big data, machine learning, and artificial intelligence tools to put the most relevant content front and center. Such tools are already being utilized by content streaming platforms, e-commerce brands, and even social media platforms to provide personalization at scale.

In Part 3 we'll discuss how event professionals can close the gap around personalized and engaging attendee experiences using examples from the dawn of the live studio audience, eSports, the NBA bubble, content streaming platforms, and original studies conducted on virtual and hybrid event programs.

People and Process

Overcoming the challenges and meeting the opportunities presented by the hybrid era will require event professionals to develop new skills and further develop some of their existing expertise.

Historically, we referred to event professionals as *planners* and *managers*, and as their titles imply, they were largely responsible for logistics. Moving forward, event professionals will still need to manage traditional responsibilities associated with in-person events, such as venue contracts, catering, travel, and budgeting, but they will also need to acquire an expanded range of capabilities. To close the Event Impact Gap™, event professionals will need to pivot their focus from the planning and coordinating of in-person events to designing experiences for a diverse, hybrid audience.

Aided by the increased availability of data and the enhanced tools at their disposal, event professionals will be better prepared to shift their focus toward outcomes and experiences. Thriving in this landscape will require new skills, new teams, and new approaches to event strategy. Event professionals will need a base level understanding of and comfort with data, sales and marketing, and digital content production. They will also need a range of soft skills like communication, collaboration, and creative problem solving.

We will dive into the new skills, new roles, and new teams that will be required to close the Event Impact Gap™ in Part 4 with the help of industry leaders behind the event strategies of brands like GitHub, IBM, Money 20/20, and Cannes-Lions.

Technology

Closing the Event Impact Gap™ and delivering a successful hybrid event will also require adopting tools and technologies that can help bring your vision to life. In this new environment, flexibility is vital, both in enabling event teams to craft a truly unique experience for their audiences and in enabling those audiences to craft their preferred multichannel attendee experience.

Up until recently, event teams had a small handful of vendors to choose from, but in the wake of the pandemic there are now a wide range of options, including some traditional incumbents, some newer start-ups, and even a few adjacent technology providers that have recently entered the events space.

Knowing whom to partner with in this more fragmented technology environment is no easy task, but it is a vital one because your virtual and hybrid events are only as powerful as the technology behind them. In Part 5 we dive into the technology landscape to help you determine which provider is best prepared to bring your vision to life, by exploring the history of event technology, how the landscape has changed in the wake of COVID-19, the questions to ask yourself before choosing an event technology partner, what features to consider, how to navigate the onboarding process, and what the future of event technology holds.

■ ■ ■

All of these changes, however, are just the tip of the iceberg. After decades (perhaps even centuries) of being relatively closed off to innovation, the live events industry is going to evolve suddenly in the short term as it catches up to the rest of the digital world—and then it will keep evolving well into the future.

It took a desperate situation, some quick thinking, and a whole lot of luck for us as a company to make that quick transition and meet the moment. Now every player in the live events industry is going to have to do the same. The old tried-and-true road map is now a relic of the past. We know we don't have all the answers, but fortunately we have developed close relationships with many thought leaders across the industry who can help show us the way. As we navigate this uncertain future, we intend to use these pages to share some of what we've learned, as well as the advice we've received from some of the brightest minds in the industry, in hopes that we can help be a guide for others as well.

PART

Data

The Age of Disruption

In the previous chapter, we outlined four challenges presented by the Event Impact Gap™—the gap between the event that event organizers want to achieve and what current tools, and knowledge with those tools, enable them to achieve.

One of these challenges is the ability to capture, connect, and leverage event leaders' most valuable customer and experience data. Key to understanding how the events industry can overcome this challenge is understanding how new technology and the data that they can surface have completely disrupted events as we know them.

Disruption is a word that gets tossed around so much in the tech industry that it's almost a joke to title a chapter about it. But the 21st century, at least up to this point, has truly been shaped by technological disruption. So much of our world has been changed so dramatically in such a short period of time that it's easy to forget how far we've come. Whatever friction you experience with a product or brand today could be solved by a start-up you've never heard of tomorrow; in 10 years, that same start-up could grow to dwarf the legacy incumbent.

We now live in an economy where just about every industry has to adapt or else risk obsolescence. The typical examples include taxis (Uber), hotels (Airbnb), music (Spotify, Apple Music), and video stores (Netflix, Apple TV, Disney+, Amazon Prime Video), but just about every industry is facing some kind of disruptive competitor—one that is using data to gain an edge on their established veterans. When people say that every company today is a tech company, what they mean is that every company needs to undergo a digital transformation and adopt a data-driven strategy in order to compete in the 21st century.

The eyewear industry—once dominated by a small handful of global conglomerates like Luxottica—is now struggling to compete with start-ups like Warby Parker. Warby Parker was founded as a website that sold prescription lenses at fair prices with a strong focus on digital marketing and email communications. They also leveraged a popular try-before-you-buy program as a way to earn consumer trust while building a database of user preferences to help inform their future selections. As of 2020, Warby Parker had 125 stores across North America and a $3 billion valuation (Crook, 2020).

Replacing razor blades and shaving accessories used to be similarly costly and inconvenient, and up until recently the industry was dominated by a small group of global players. Today, subscription services like Harry's, which was recently valued at $1.7 billion (Bertoni, 2021), and Dollar Shave Club, which was sold to Unilever in 2016 for $1 billion (CNBC, 2019), use data to build online communities around shaving and grooming with millions of members.

Even grocery stores and gas stations offer incentives and rewards programs that collect data and tailor their experiences to the individual consumer, with deals and promotions that respond to consumer shopping habits. Whether in banking or education, prescription medication or insurance, the prevailing theme of the 21st century is that the organizations that best utilize data to improve the customer experience win the day.

This trend of offering bespoke services at scale is often referred to as *mass personalization*, and we believe this is where the event industry is heading.

For example, the team behind Salesforce's Dreamforce uses behavioral data from its virtual events to say, "Hey attendee, I saw you do A; I think maybe you should go watch B," explained Salesforce's Rexson Serrao on an episode of the IN-PERSON podcast published in June 2021. "I think the future of personalization is really merging it with this idea of journey." From before the event begins to while it's happening to after the event concludes, organizers should tailor the experience of attendees based on their unique interests and needs. Otherwise, "you're missing an opportunity to take them on their personal journey with your brand."

In other words, data is and will continue to shape the experiences we provide to attendees—before, during, and after the event day.

Looking back at our example of data disruptors (Spotify, Airbnb, Netflix, Amazon, etc.), we see that industry heavyweights that believe they are immune to personalization are eventually (and inevitably) proven wrong, while those that see the writing on the wall and adapt accordingly ultimately thrive. Data, when gathered, stored, and utilized properly, can help businesses of all shapes and sizes improve the customer experience, streamline their internal processes, and improve a wide array of business outcomes.

This pattern has been repeated countless times in a range of industries in recent decades, yet ours has largely remained immune to such changes—at least, until now.

The current evolution of data collection and utilization has the potential to elevate events from a standalone channel and a "black box" of data to a powerful insight generator for digital marketers, sales teams, executives, and other stakeholders. In contrast to its previous standing as a team that was overlooked in the past, events have become much more of a priority because of the never-before-seen data that we're now able to utilize.

As Devin Cleary—who led event programs at HubSpot and served as vice president of experiential marketing at the enterprise software firm PTC before joining Bizzabo as vice president of global events in March 2021—puts it, "Each event is a moment in time where you've got the largest pool of people together, and you're able to engage your audience and test out new ideas.

As a result, events are able to surface data on attendees that other teams within organizations would otherwise not have access to."

The Attendee Experience

Whether they're conscious of it or not, attendees, sponsors, exhibitors, speakers, and other stakeholders put up with a lot of inconveniences when they attended events in the past, inconveniences they were trained not to accept elsewhere. After all, if your local café allows you to order ahead on an app to avoid waiting in a short line to pay for your coffee, why should you spend hours in line to get a good seat at the conference keynote?

"There is an expectation for a consumer-grade experience, and events have been anything but in the past," explains Nicola Kastner, vice president and global head of event strategy at SAP. "We are sophisticated digital consumers in our personal lives, but we check those expectations at the door when we go to an event; we're okay with a less than seamless experience. Standing in line to register, standing in line to check into the hotel, trying to figure out how to build your calendar, and then making sure your mobile app is working—it's overwhelming."

Nicola suggests that enhanced customer experiences tied to countless everyday products and services have raised the bar on consumer expectations. Previously, when it came to events, these inconveniences were excused as part of the trade-off. Attendees generally believed that events were worth the time, money, and headaches that came with them.

According to Nicola, after more than a year of attending events virtually—thus avoiding those inconveniences—many attendees will begin to question that tradeoff and demand a more personalized, efficient, and convenient experience in the future.

"What we're realizing is that the stagnation, the consistency, and the staleness that was ongoing prior to the pandemic, that can't reemerge," adds Devin Cleary. "If companies choose that route in terms of the safety play, they are not going to be around much longer; their consumers are going to choose competitors to invest their time in, because they are trying to meet them halfway, where their customers are, in the format, style, and duration they prefer."

As we discussed in Part 1, the industry has long been immune to the forces of disruption that have upended countless other businesses in the past 10 or 20 years because the model works naturally; if you put buyers and sellers in a room together, business outcomes will flow.

According to entrepreneur and events industry veteran Marco Giberti, "Even if you don't do a fantastic data job pre- and post-event, if you facilitate those connections face-to-face, most likely your community will say it was a great investment of [their] time and money; they'll come back next year because the human connection face-to-face is such a powerful thing that it adds tremendous speed into the deal nurturing and closing in comparison to other tools. That's why the industry was, in some way, reasonably isolated from digital transformation and digital disruption—because the model works."

Business-to-business (B2B) events have always been about relationship building—and that won't change any time soon. But with the rise of virtual and hybrid events, and the data they yield, we are seeing new ways to expedite that process and increase the value each attendee extracts from their participation.

Just as attendees stand to benefit from this evolution of data spurred by hybrid event strategies, so do event experience leaders and the organizations they are a part of.

As Marco puts it, "If in the past your strategy was 10,000 people in Vegas once a year, in the future it's going to be 2,000 people in Vegas once a year, 500 people in three cities, and 10 virtual events.

And because of that combination of data knowledge and activation, your job and your budget and your return on investment will be significantly better than in the past. That's the potential big change that we're going to see in the future because of the crash course we just had during COVID, moving everything virtual."

In fact, many event organizers are already seeing the benefits of increased data accessibility and utilization. Take, for example, the events team at the AI technology and enablement firm DataRobot, which used real-time analytics to streamline its virtual attendee experience and leveraged its event platform's Salesforce integration to make decisions about future events. The company was able to use insights like who stayed for the shortest or longest amount of time to determine which attendees would be best primed for event follow-up as potential customers and which sessions were most relevant to their audience.

Through the process of digital transformation, events are becoming more cost-effective, more effective in achieving stated outcomes, more integrated with digital marketing efforts, more demonstrably valuable to organizations that host events, and better positioned to offer a better, more personalized experience for attendees. Moving forward, CMOs and marketers will expect to be able to measure the return on events (ROE) at an even more granular level. Attendees will expect a personalized experience that maximizes the time and resources they dedicate to events. Sponsors will demand better insights into their audiences to target their messaging more effectively.

Fortunately, as we saw with the events team at DataRobot, we as an industry already have a head start. Unlike Warby Parker or Harry's or even Netflix, we are approaching the starting line of this digital transformation journey with a trove of data, a network of engaged users, and buy-in from decision-makers. All we need now are event organizers who understand the fundamentals of how to collect, store, and utilize that data effectively.

The Event Data Maturity Curve

From our perspective, the biggest gift the pandemic offered was furthering the events industry along the **event data maturity curve**, a framework for understanding how the industry has progressed toward maximizing the value of data.

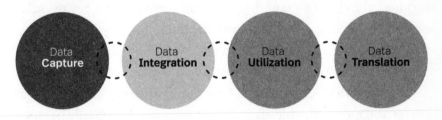

Identifying the Four Steps of Event Data Maturity

Events have long stagnated behind most other industries in the use of data, but they are finally starting to catch up. The first step in the event data maturity curve is improving the availability of data, which is more robust today thanks to holistic tools, event applications, and the digitization of events in general. We call this step **data capture**. Event organizers can see which sessions an attendee signs up for and which company an attendee represents. Email marketers can see which contacts open their emails and which links they click in those emails (if any). In short, because of the availability of more technologies and their growing sophistication, we now have a lot more data to work with.

The second step in the event data maturity curve for event organizers is to connect that data to business systems—such as customer relationship management (CRM) platforms, the sales technology stack, digital marketing platforms, and association management systems—in order to enrich those systems. We call this step **data integration**. Insights into attendees and their actions—such as the type of people they interact with, the types of sessions they attend, and how engaged they are in those sessions—will help paint a picture of customer intent.

Intent data is the holy grail of B2B event insights and is traditionally very hard to extract. As Nicola described it, "Understanding when somebody is showing a buying signal from a product they don't own" has tremendous value in aiding sales efforts. As we move further along the data maturity curve, events will emerge as a powerful source of data that can help convert prospects and upsell existing customers.

Part of that same process includes utilizing data to offer better and more valuable attendee experiences. To actually personalize events to the point where 5,000 attendees can have 5,000 unique experiences is still an aspiration more than a reality, but we're finally moving in the right direction.

In order to achieve those attendee experience and business outcome goals, organizers need to master the next step of the event data maturity curve: the ability to identify and curate the precise data points that can help achieve those goals. We call this **data utilization**. It's one thing to plug your event data into your business management systems; it's another to ensure that it's capturing and analyzing useful data that can enrich those systems. Moving from the first stage of data capture to the stage of data utilization is no small feat, but new tools and platforms will help ease the transition.

The final step in the event data maturity curve is translating those data points into **insights**. On the attendee side, this data can help you improve the event experience in a number of ways. For instance, if you discover that 40 percent of your attendees are young, early-career professionals, you can tailor the content and agenda accordingly. If you were to gain better insights into why attendees choose your event over your competitors, you can lean into those key features. If you discover that 30 percent of your attendees are traveling to your event in the United States from Asia, it might make sense to host a standalone event that caters to that market specifically.

Improving the attendee experience will ultimately help drive ROE. If you can increase engagement in a measurable way—if you can curate experiences that speak to each attendee—attendees are far more likely to find value in attending and return year after year.

If you were to ask the average person what their best experience was at any event they've attended, the answers might range from meeting the person who changed their career trajectory to a meeting privately with a keynote speaker. Everyone who attends events on a regular basis has a few highlights that stand out above the rest, and they are much more likely to return to the events that facilitated them. If you can drive more of those experiences, if you can find out what gets people most excited and offer it to them on a consistent basis, you can create a loyal and engaged event attendee.

Using Data to Make Events Outcome-Oriented

Improving the event experience goes hand in hand with improving event outcomes. As we move along the maturity curve, outcomes will eventually be designed into the fabric of event experiences from day one. In other words, a specific event will be designed to achieve a specific outcome among a specific group of participants, optimized and measured every step of the way.

Looking a little further off into the future, this data will eventually allow an AI engine to help event experience leaders design events to achieve specific outcomes. We imagine a world where you can plug in your objectives, budget, target audience, and a few other data points and have an automated system recommend the appropriate event size, venue, host city, speakers, activations, and playbooks you can draw on. Just as an AI engine could inform decisions of how to design an event, so could it inform decisions around which accounts, attendees, sponsors, or exhibitors to target and the type of content that will help drive specific outcomes across that group.

This isn't a matter of science fiction, but rather a matter of data maturity, and we're already making significant strides in the right direction. Over time we will have enough data to train an AI system to provide these types of recommendations. It won't be easy, but it's absolutely within the realm of possibility. After all, plenty of other industries are already able to do this effectively, including entertainment (Netflix), e-commerce (Amazon), and social media (Facebook).

6

Reaching the Right Audience at the Right Time

The dizzying array of potential opportunities to collect and utilize data can be intimidating to the uninitiated, but understanding data's potential is vital for event experience managers in the age of disruption.

The transformation that the events industry is about to undertake is not unlike the one that advertising went through in the mid-1990s, as it made the jump from television, radio, billboards, and fliers to digital advertising channels like banner ads and social media content.

As with most jumps from the physical to the virtual world, digital advertising began by taking traditional ad content and simply moving it online. Instead of posting a billboard on the side of a highway, early digital advertising sought to place a version of that same billboard at the top of a popular web page. The key difference was that users could interact with the ad. Specifically, they could click on it in order to be taken to the advertisers' website or landing page.

The first banner ad was launched on October 27, 1994, on a website called HotWired, *Wired* magazine's online offshoot at the time. The website charged advertisers an upfront fee to place a banner ad on the site for three months, similar to a traditional magazine or billboard ad.

Soon after, advertisers realized that they didn't need to serve the same ad to every single visitor on the website; they could actually increase the effectiveness of each advertisement they served by targeting specific consumer demographics. In 1995, Boca Raton, Florida–based digital ad agency WebConnect began helping clients identify their ideal customers' online activity, and only served ads to users who met certain criteria. The company also allowed its clients to set a limit on how many times a particular user was shown the same ad. After all, if the user didn't click on the ad the first 10 times they saw it, why should they pay for the 11th?

Then in 1996, New York City–based digital advertising agency DoubleClick launched a new and revolutionary service that would allow advertisers to track not only how many people viewed a specific ad on a specific website, but how many times the same ad was seen and clicked on across multiple websites. This allowed advertisers to track the effectiveness of their ad across the Internet in real time and make changes to their campaigns to optimize their returns. If an ad was performing well with a certain demographic, or on a certain type of website, the advertiser could change its visibility accordingly, and thus improve their return on investment. This process gave way to a new and more dynamic pricing model and introduced the concept of cost per mille (CPM, a thousand impressions).

Through the mid-2000s, with the rise of social media and online search platforms, advertisers had new ways of reaching the right audiences with the right messaging at the right time. The trove of data that became available about each individual user through increased online activity made it easier to target ads accordingly. Now advertisers had the tools to serve ads only to those who were most likely to convert into a sale, on the platform that was most likely to reach them, using the most effective messaging for that user type. Today, digital advertising has come to be seen as more valuable than traditional advertising for its ability to effectively target the users, to be flexible and adaptable in real time, and (ultimately) to improve ROI.

What took the advertising industry a quarter of a century to achieve is now being pursued by the events industry in a much more condensed time frame, as the desire to leverage data effectively is likewise unfolding.

According to a study we conducted in 2019, 60 percent of enterprise leaders believe events are the most critical marketing channel for achieving business goals, but 54 percent struggle to prove their return on investment. The event success strategy of the past involved gathering a large audience and exposing them all to the same messaging, not unlike traditional advertisements.

Like the switch from billboards to banner ads, the transition from entirely in-person events to hybrid and virtual events will generate valuable data and insights about user behaviors that will serve to improve their performance. Using data, events themselves will become as targeted as online ads.

The days of simply accepting that events work without any means of measuring and optimizing their performance—accepting the "black box" as fact—are over. In its wake will be a new era of events, one that similarly targets the right users with the right messaging at the right time to optimize and improve ROE.

Informing Event Strategy

Let's take a basic example that will be familiar to organizers in every category. Let's say you're running a flagship event in three weeks and only 40 percent of your attendees from the previous year have registered. At this point, you just might be on the verge of panicking—until you go back into the data from previous years and find that 60 percent of your registrations typically occur in the two weeks before the event. Knowing that information can give you some peace of mind and prevent you from making any rash decisions before the anticipated spike.

Now let's say you want to break that pattern next year, so you start looking at the data from previous years and find that only 10 percent of registrants take advantage of early bird ticket sales. With this insight in mind, you can begin to investigate why.

With just a small amount of data about registration patterns, coupled with some insights into your target market, you could solve a major challenge for your event. Perhaps your early bird pricing isn't enticing enough to attendees, and so you decide to lower the price. Perhaps your early bird sale isn't being advertised effectively, and in post-event surveys you discover that a majority of your attendees weren't aware such a sale existed, so you decide to run a marketing campaign to advertise the sale next year. Perhaps the data suggests that your audience members typically don't pay for their own registrations and don't really care about the price. One outcome from this analysis may be that you decide to offer exclusive perks to your first 100 registrants, like a backstage pass with the keynote speaker, in order to drive up that early bird registration.

While this data was available to event organizers in the pre-COVID era, the type of data and insights that became available during the pandemic—through the emergence of the virtual and hybrid events coupled with new tools for capturing and analyzing data—will take data-driven decision-making to another level.

Take, for instance, the events team at DJI, the world's largest consumer and enterprise drone company. In 2020, the team pivoted their annual AirWorks conference to virtual for the first time ever. The team was naturally cautious about how the virtual experience would support their goals of driving attendee experience, promoting community building, and creating an effortless speaker and sponsor experience. However, the experience turned out to be a boon not only for driving their main goals but gathering data in the process. Using Bizzabo's reporting tools, the DJI team was able to learn who purchased tickets, where they were purchasing them from, who showed up, and other details about their attendees. Using this information, the DJI team was able to surpass their registration goal of 850 by almost 39 percent and saw that between live attendees and on-demand viewers, nearly 73 percent of registrants converted to virtual attendees.

In the words of one team member, "[This] was the first time we've ever had this kind of information for this event. To then go virtual and be able to really home in on who is attending, at what time, and who tuned in live or on-demand—that data was more robust than anything that we've had before."

Targeting Key Accounts

Sophisticated data insights and analytics tools can today help corporate marketers learn where a particular prospect is in their buyer's journey (their path toward purchase) and organize event experiences specifically based on those stages. Taking this concept a step further, many companies today choose to put additional resources behind a number of key accounts. Especially in the enterprise B2B space, we believe events will become more integrated with sales and marketing teams tasked with pursuing these key accounts.

Consider the reemerging importance of account-based marketing (ABM) strategies that require an intimate understanding of the target account's needs, their key decision-makers, and how to reach them effectively. In ABM, marketers assign scores to various accounts that represent where they are in their buyer's journey and then serve content based on those scores. ABM can be done in a one-to-many approach where similar accounts receive similar content based on their collective qualities, or ABM can be done in a more focused one-to-one approach where unique accounts receive content that is tailor-made to them. The common analogy is that, rather than casting a wide net, ABM is like fishing with a spear. According to one study (Demandbase, 2022), the average annual contract value

(ACV) for account-based marketing deals is 33 percent higher on average than non-ABM deals.

Armed with an ABM approach and the right data to support it, event organizers can be even more targeted and intentional with their events strategy and create personalized content for that specific client or prospect. While this has applications for creating curated experiences at large conferences where those who attend may be across the spectrum of the buyer's journey, it also has applications for smaller bespoke experiences that are focused on nurturing prospects toward closing business—this is called **field marketing**.

As Nani Shaffer (former vice president of account-based marketing at Demandbase) shared with us on an episode of the IN-PERSON podcast published in March 2020, "Field marketing is often looking through the same lens as sales, so they make a natural combo there that lends itself well to an ABM strategy."

Corporate events—whether field marketing events or large conferences—can be vital in gathering the necessary data to better understand clients, as well as being one of the channels used to reach them. With some basic information about decision-makers' actions and behaviors at an event, marketers can better determine how to reach them based on what content they engage with, who they are meeting with, and how they prefer to be reached.

Improving Attendee Engagement and Communication

Post-event communications is an important touchpoint for turning attendees into prospects and prospects into sales, but that communication is only as valuable as the data informing it. Previously, in the best-case scenario, organizers could tailor their post-event messaging to attendees based on registration data and post-event surveys, but the data wasn't always accurate.

For example, let's say an attendee at a technology conference is asked three months prior to the event what their main area of interest is and clicks on "mixed reality." When the event rolls around, however, the data shows that the person attended 14 total sessions with only one session specific to mixed reality and the remaining 13 focused on artificial intelligence. At the end of that event, organizers would be much better served following up with a webinar on artificial intelligence delivered by one of the speakers at the event rather than with an e-book on mixed reality.

With the right tools, events can become powerful data generators for sales and marketing teams, critical channels for reaching targeted audiences, and effective pathways to community growth.

7

SAPPHIRE NOW:
A Case Study in Event Data
Utilization

You may not have heard of SAP, but you've almost certainly encountered its products. In fact, it is estimated that 77 percent of the world's transaction revenue comes into contact with SAP's software.

Founded in Weinheim, Germany, in 1972 by former IBM engineers, SAP is considered a pioneer of digital accounting, payroll, and production planning systems for IT departments. As of 2021, the company had a market capitalization of more than $162 billion, over 335,000 customers spread across 180 countries, and a spot on the Fortune 500 list.

SAP runs thousands of events on just about every corner of the globe each year, but is widely known for its flagship event SAPPHIRE NOW, which welcomes 24,000 customers, prospects, and partners to Orlando, Florida, each spring. According to Nicola Kastner, SAP's vice president and global head of event strategy, the event is by far the company's largest pipeline generator.

In 2019, Nicola was promoted into a new role where she was tasked with refining the company's event portfolio and providing a different perspective on the flagship event. It was the perfect union between a company that runs on data and a professional who has always maintained a data-first approach to event strategy.

"My approach to data has been a career differentiator," says Nicola. "I never considered myself an analytical person in the past, like when I was in school, but when I understood that data could provide so many insights early on in my career, it literally changed my trajectory away from being an event planner—or in the event business, so to speak—to being a business strategist."

When SAPPHIRE NOW hosted its first iteration nearly 30 years ago, it was designed to sell on-premise **enterprise resource planning (ERP)** systems to IT departments. ERP systems manage day-to-day business activities like accounting, procurement, project management, risk management and compliance, and supply chain operations.

Each year SAPPHIRE NOW occupies roughly one million square feet of the Orange County Convention Center in Orlando for three days, with every element of the event (aside from its closing concert) taking place in one centralized location. That includes a meeting center with 252 rooms, customer showcases, demo stations, a partner expo, keynote stage, and food and beverage—all under the same roof.

When Nicola took the helm of this monumental event, she sought to maintain a customer-first, outcome-oriented approach, informed by data. She saw the event as a way to solve real customer needs while seamlessly integrating it into the customer journey. SAP no longer just sells its solutions to the IT industry. Its enterprise intelligence software is utilized in a range of departments across almost every industry.

Not long after the 2019 event, on an episode of Bizzabo's IN-PERSON podcast in October that same year, Nicola shared with us that she started by considering who came to the event and why. Nicola explains that the process began with segmenting audience members into personas, including their department; what products they currently own; the type of business, industry, or vertical they operate in; and so on. From those insights, she distilled SAPPHIRE NOW into five overarching themes, as she explains:

If you think about SAP and 77 percent of the world's business transactions operating on our platforms, that's a lot of industries, a lot of customers. And so we needed to think about what was a common foundation for all of these different customers, and industries, and segments, and so forth. And we realized that accelerating changes in the economy, society, and the environment were affecting every single company, no matter their size, geography, or industry. And because of those changes, all of our customers were dealing with macro issues. The same issues. Maybe not all of the same issues to the same degree, but dealing with these five macro issues: *business model disruption, data proliferation, empowered customers, a diverse workforce,* and *resource scarcity.* Every company—no matter their industry, size, or geography—is dealing with those things. And they're impacting all areas of the business as well, not just IT, not just marketing, everywhere.

In order to bring these concepts into a real-world environment, Nicola and her team presented them as five neighborhoods spread across the exhibition floor, each focused on one of the macro issues customers of all shapes and sizes were trying to solve. Each neighborhood had its own design concept, content, demos, networking spaces—even food and beverage. "In a neighborhood, people live, work, and play, and that's exactly what we wanted to do and capture within the SAPPHIRE NOW show floor design," she said.

Nicola goes on to explain that if an attendee is really focused on a single challenge, they could spend all three days in that neighborhood. And, like a real city, each was separated by soft borders where neighborhoods would blend, further facilitating exploration.

The event was so successful that it was awarded the 2019 BizBash Event Style Award for the Best Corporate Event Concept in the $500,000+ budget category.

From Grocery Stores to Meal Delivery Services

Nicola explains that activations and programming were informed by an ABM approach, in partnership and coordination with sales and marketing teams. Nicola likens it to evolving from a grocery store, where patrons walk around checking off items on their list, to a meal kit delivery service, where customers are proactively offered the ingredients they need.

"ABM is a big part of our marketing strategy and a huge part of the approach that we take within the event. Because we have key customers that we want there, we have plans that are developed against those customers," she shared. "Specific customer activities and programming are created by our sales team and our ABM marketing managers specifically around SAPPHIRE, utilizing that as a tool as part of the entire ABM strategy."

For example, if a current customer account running SAP's HR solutions registered for event sessions and demos related to its procurement solution set, SAP could engage with that customer accordingly. "We saw their buying behaviors; we could tell when somebody was showing a buying signal from a product they don't own," Nicola says.

Nicola adds that the organization also sets goals for registration percentages among the top target accounts in certain key regions, with each region carrying its own specific quotas. Furthermore, SAP puts tools and assets in place to enable the customer success teams to invite their target accounts to the event and designs customized experiences for each one. The company also utilizes a digital listening engine that includes internal and external data to identify those accounts that are most likely to be making purchasing decisions and crafts custom journeys within the events, as well as through other marketing touch points.

Like most other in-person events, the 2020 iteration of SAPPHIRE NOW, which was scheduled for May of that year, had to be canceled. And like most of the industry at the time, Nicola took the temporary pause as an opportunity to reflect on the state of events and consider how best to facilitate those business outcomes in the future. She was kind enough to outline some of her thoughts to us (over Zoom, of course) from her home just outside of Toronto in April 2021:

> We really took a step back and said, "What are the right things we need to know about our customers that will help us drive value for them?" So imagine when you can connect all of those different pieces of data together, the impact that it can have for the business. But most companies don't, because it's too difficult to get beyond silos. So what's the source of truth? CRM [customer relationship management], which is maintained by sales? Or is it a shared view of data, where you're taking all of the right insights. Who owns the data? How does the data get updated? Those are critical conversations that have to happen now, because of this abundance of data that we're receiving, and a customer expectation that we know them.

Nicola has been able to drive real, measurable business results for SAP through its flagship events in no small part because she approaches events as a data-first, business outcome-oriented, and customer-focused initiative.

We see Nicola as an **event experience leader**—someone who is committed to delivering experiences that overcome the Event Impact Gap™ and drive business impact across virtual, in-person, and hybrid events. "In a hybrid environment we have the opportunity to target the right event type, at the right time, for the right customers, and I believe that when physical events come back, a highly targeted ABM approach will be a core part of the strategy for many companies," she says.

Closing the Event Impact Gap™ with Data

Of course, not everyone has the resources of a Fortune 500 company or the luxury of working for a company that was built on data and analytics. Today, there remains a significant gap between most professionals who run events and the rest of the organization, but our goal as a company is to democratize those resources and make them accessible to every organizer.

Closing the Event Impact Gap™, which prevents many organizers from being able to definitively demonstrate the value of their efforts, will go a long way in encouraging organizations to dedicate more resources to their events. Furthermore, as we emerge from the pandemic and into a hybrid-focused future, that gap will be simpler to close because of the vast number of data points that will become available. We believe that in the near future, events will play an even more critical role in ABM and marketing, organizational, and stakeholder strategies.

Nicola says that moving forward, customers will prefer smaller, more targeted events, though she believes SAPPHIRE NOW will continue on as a three-day event that blends in-person and virtual experiences and that it will remain a rallying point for SAP customers and partners year-round. The key transition she envisions for the industry coming out of the pandemic is the change from seeing events as a standalone and somewhat mysterious corner of the marketing strategy to being an important partner in facilitating the customer journey. According to Nicola:

Events are one channel, and no one channel can ever claim responsibility or success for driving a customer relationship. If events are just one channel that is integrated with all other marketing channels, and other channels outside of marketing, that extends into a 365 omnichannel journey that adds value to our customers. You can look at it both ways; an integrated data strategy is going to drive that 365 omnichannel view of the customer, or the 365 omnichannel view of the customer that is required and expected is going to drive data integration; either way, the outcome is the same in my mind.

The pandemic undoubtedly created a lot of hardship for the events industry and the ecosystem that surrounds it, but it also provided the push the industry needed to achieve its full potential in the Digital Age. Nicola believes that the industry has been presented with a unique opportunity to reinvent itself, using the wide range of new tools and capabilities that have found their way into most other parts of the business world:

As an industry we've fallen in love with the solution, not the problem we've been trying to solve. When you think about the events industry, we've had incremental change. We are now at a point where the industry has been revolutionized for us, and I often say it's the gift we didn't know we wanted, from an industry perspective. I think that we benchmarked success on the wrong things—the size of events, not audience value. So I think as we come back we have to think about what success looks like in a completely different way.

CHAPTER

8

With New Data Power Comes New Responsibility

The data revolution currently taking place in the events industry will offer organizers new capabilities to personalize engagement and curate experiences. But with this new capacity comes a duty of care—one that must be shared by organizers, their technology partners, and the industry as a whole.

Protecting User Data

First and foremost, organizers have a responsibility to protect the data and privacy of attendees. In some cases that might include abiding by international data standards, like the European Union's General Data Protection Regulation (GDPR), and in others it may require surpassing them by prescribing privacy protections that have yet to be written into law.

In this context, the event industry is not unique. At a certain point all industries that have been revolutionized by data have had to address data privacy issues. The highly fragmented nature of the event ecosystem, however, can create some additional problems for event organizers when it comes to remaining compliant with GDPR and providing stakeholders with confidence that their personal information is being protected.

"Big organizers are not using one or two technologies on their shows; big organizers are using on average 15 to 20 different technologies per show," says Marco. "That means each technology activation is a potential challenge, and organizers need to make sure that every one of those technologies is solid, serious, and respectful of data privacy."

One solution for event organizers is to have a stated policy regarding how attendee data is managed (most do) and to be transparent with attendees about the kinds of data you're collecting on them (and why), as well as offering the opportunity to opt out. Furthermore, users shouldn't have to go digging for that information or jump through hoops in order to opt out; it should be explained, in plain language, followed by a clear choice between opting in and opting out. We feel that this above-and-beyond level of transparency is vital in today's world of tech-savvy consumers.

Another way for organizers to live up to their data privacy promises is to select technology partners whose data privacy policies align with theirs. In GDPR parlance, software providers, referred to as data *processors* (as opposed to *organizers*, who are considered data *controllers*), pledge that all the data that is gathered from attendees at their events remains in the organizer's control. It also means that technology firms agree not to use data collected on behalf of organizers for direct marketing to attendees or to enable derivative products or services that the partner might be interested in developing.

Testing Organizer Resolve

Of course, these alliances between organizers and technology providers are being managed in an environment that remains fluid. Not all event technology firms are on board with these types of data concessions. Plus, leading technology companies are in the process of restricting the amount of data that digital platforms (including virtual events) can collect from users.

For example, at the start of the pandemic there were very few restrictions on adding cookies to browsers. Organizers could track the attendee's journey across an events platform, from the sessions they attended and the length of time they spent viewing presentations to the advertisements they were served and whether they clicked on them. One year later, both Apple and Google have announced plans to effectively remove those capabilities on iPhones and the Google Chrome web browser. These restrictions can effectively prevent organizers from tracking their attendees' end-to-end journey across the event marketing tech stack.

These changes will undoubtedly serve to slow the industry's progress along the data maturity curve, but they will also serve as an important litmus test on organizers' relationships with their communities.

As Devin Cleary puts it, "When there's the possibility of so much data, and then it starts to get restricted, this is the test that says, 'Do we truly have the followers and the fans and the community that we think we have?' If we do then they'll go along with authorizing us, every single time, to take that data. And they'll do so because we've made it clear what we do with the data, and they trust us."

While organizers devise ways to protect data privacy, they also have to manage data security. Recent years have seen countless exposés, documentaries, and feature stories about all the ways users are tracked and followed on their devices, and how even the most secure organizations—banks, defense departments, government institutions—are not immune to cyberattacks and data breaches.

After more than a decade of unfettered access to their data, consumers are waking up to the dark side of the data economy and demanding more from the technology platforms that collect them. Again, the appropriate vetting of technology partners will help organizers protect customers and meet their growing security expectations.

In addition to privacy concerns, the event industry must also grapple with the issue of **data silos**, which the organization behind VSef, a universal data format for hybrid and virtual events, describes as "pots of data that don't talk to each other or contribute to wider business insight" (VSef, 2021). Silos prevent organizers from analyzing data from multiple virtual platforms and transferring it into other business systems, such as CRMs, marketing automation, and other components of the marketing technology stack.

"If we don't find a way to collaborate on data exchange and data capture in a way that's easy for everyone, it's going to take a long time before it's relevant for the organizers," explains Marco Giberti. "If you go from one vendor to the other and you're unable to capture data and consolidate data with formats that are standard—as you can see in other industries—if we don't have something like that in the event industry, it's going to be difficult."

The industry's data silo problem has far-reaching implications. Silos make data more vulnerable and less useful. Breaking down those data silos between vendors and organizers, and between the events industry and other sales and marketing platforms, would enable the industry to share benchmarks and KPIs as an events community, provide a more personalized attendee experience, become better integrated into ABM strategy, close the Event Impact Gap™, and ultimately drive higher ROE.

Despite these challenges, the industry is still much further along than it would have been without the pandemic. Across industries, event organizers are beginning to take a harder look at data utilization and the potential for collaboration.

Audience Engagement

CHAPTER

9

Engagement in a Hybrid Era

We were already living in a hybrid world before the pandemic moved most business online, even if we didn't notice it at the time. When you ordered a ride or a snack using an app, when you watched the first few minutes of a soccer match at a sports bar before taking your seat in the stadium, when you checked out a movie preview on your phone on the way to the theater, when everyone in the conference room worked off of the same Google doc from their own devices, you were engaging in a hybrid experience. When executed effectively, this blending of in-person and virtual experiences is so seamless we don't even notice the transitions between them.

In recent years, the most popular products and the most innovative companies have found harmony at the intersection of physical and digital, enabling them to deliver more personalized, more connected, more impactful, and more *human* experiences.

Even in the events space, live experiences have long been augmented by virtual tools that enable further engagement. Attendees often purchase their tickets online, conduct research into speakers and events, and build their schedules before the event begins. On the ground they use their devices to check into venues, scan their tickets, respond to polls, enter contests, ask questions, post pictures and videos online, and message fellow attendees. After the event they are encouraged to continue those conversations online, connect with new contacts on social networks, and fill out surveys about their experience.

As we emerge on the other side of the pandemic, technology will only further enable the blending of these two worlds. Event organizers spent the last year thinking of in-person and online as two separate venues, but the post-pandemic era of events will be defined by more purposeful and more seamless integration of the two. We will call it *hybrid*; our attendees will just call it "an event," much in the same way that we don't call paying our bills online "Internet banking" anymore.

In this hybrid world, simply livestreaming the keynote presentation won't cut it; in the coming years organizers will be tasked with improving the digital event experience by taking a more creative and personalized approach to engaging their audiences.

By now everyone has heard of Zoom fatigue. But according to J. Damany Daniel, the chief imaginator at The EventNerd, presenters of business-to-consumer (B2C) digital content do not tend to have the same problem. "Zoom fatigue is a real thing. We are on Zoom calls all day, every day. Zoom fatigue is a diagnosed condition," he said in November 2020. "But you know what is not a diagnosed condition? ESPN fatigue or Netflix fatigue....You know why? They tell better stories" (Szewczyk, 2021).

Overcoming the virtual engagement gap is vital in a hybrid environment, where a large proportion of the audience can close the session with a single mouse click. While leisure travel is expected to make a roaring comeback after the pandemic, business travel is projected to lag well behind in the coming years, according to a recent McKinsey study. McKinsey estimates that business travel will likely reach only 80 percent of pre-pandemic levels by the year 2024, in large part due to the rise of remote work. That means virtual attendees will continue to dominate the events space for the foreseeable future, while in-person attendees will need to demonstrate real value to their organizations in order to justify the investment of time and resources.

Improving Virtual Engagement in a Hybrid World

To make hybrid events a success, organizers need to find a way to close the virtual engagement gap—to create business-to-business

(B2B) experiences that rival business-to-consumer virtual experiences in their ability to grab the attention of viewers and connect them to the content at hand. It won't be an easy transition for those who have dedicated their careers to engaging B2B in-person audiences.

Fortunately, through the experimentation that was necessary as a result of the pandemic, several best practices have emerged. From the first live studio audiences to the NBA bubble, there are now plenty of examples that can serve as inspiration for event organizers as they seek to solve the virtual event engagement gap.

Some of the most important engagement principles to keep in mind when organizing events in a hybrid environment include format, content, community, and experience design. We have provided a few examples of how each of these principles have been implemented in the events industry and beyond.

Format

In the era of hybrid events, organizers will be tasked with matching the right audience with the right format. Prior to the pandemic, there was really only one event format, but now there is a spectrum of options: completely virtual events, completely in-person events, and hybrid experiences that fall somewhere in-between.

The television industry is well accustomed to creating a live, in-person event designed to facilitate an at-home experience. TV shows have utilized live studio audiences since *I Love Lucy* premiered in 1951. The show's creator, Desi Arnaz, understood how those laughing and clapping along in the studio enhanced the at-home viewing audience experience. *I Love Lucy* was also innovative for essentially inventing the multi-cam sitcom format, allowing for what was at the time an unprecedented mix of live laughter and dynamic camera angles. The show's multi-cam solution is still used in variety shows and late-night TV to this day, continuing to offer a strong example of how presentation can be optimized for both in-studio and at-home audiences simultaneously.

In the coming years, event organizers are going to have to consider how to present information in a real-world setting that serves to enhance the at-home viewing experience as well. In some cases, that could mean interactive stages and even set changes, better camera angles, and enhanced lighting. It means can't-miss moments of surprise and wonder, putting added pressure on hosts and moderators, who will be responsible for building the energy of the crowd.

While the possibilities are endless for event formats that exist along this spectrum, we believe four hybrid models, in particular, are helpful for event strategists to consider:

1. **Two simultaneous events:** This model features two concurrent networking and content streaming experiences that are unified by theme, content, and timing.

2. **Delayed events:** This model features a live in-person event for attendees that is then later packaged and served to virtual audiences for on-demand viewing.

3. **Live studio audience events:** This model features a limited in-person experience, consisting of an audience and speakers, which is then streamed live to virtual attendees.

4. **Speaker-only events:** This model is similar to the live studio audience model but removes the element of the in-person audience so that only the speaker's content is presented to a virtual-only audience.

In some cases, an event may consist of sessions or moments that combine a variety of these models. Each event format on this spectrum comes with a range of advantages and disadvantages.

It is therefore vital for organizers to understand the value each can provide and align the format to the outcomes they are trying to achieve.

For instance, the reach of virtual-first experiences presents an advantage for organizers looking to drive top-of-the-funnel activity—that is, activity around lead generation or brand awareness that is targeted at prospects who are earlier in the buyer's journey.

As prospects continue their path on the buyer's journey, becoming more committed to potentially investing in your product, there is often greater value in providing a more bespoke, intimate, and exclusive in-person experience. That in-person experience could be a small-scale in-person-only event for existing customers within a certain industry and a certain geographical area or even an intimate dinner with a few choice prospects.

Whatever model you choose for your event should be dictated by attendees and sponsors and should cater to your community's needs and preferences—alongside the outcomes that you and your organization intend to drive.

Content

In-person events have a lot to offer beyond what's said on stage. Attendees spend significant time and resources to attend events for networking and sales opportunities, to engage with their community, to enjoy new and exciting experiences, and to be surprised and delighted. Unfortunately, those aspects are difficult to replicate online, at least for now.

For example, several event technology companies are investing in AI tools that can help facilitate virtual networking, but we don't anticipate audiences buying a ticket for the opportunity to network over a web camera just yet. Until something changes, content will remain the primary value proposition for remote audiences.

Nobody suffers from fatigue when presented with truly engaging content. On the contrary, we struggle to peel ourselves away from the computer screen when caught in a content binge. No matter how much you improve the presentation, format, and interactivity of hybrid events, they fall flat without truly engaging content. In the past, content sometimes took a back seat at in-person events, but content must take center stage—literally and figuratively—in a hybrid world.

Netflix, YouTube, and TikTok aren't addictive because they serve up the same pieces of content to anyone who logs on. Not everyone likes the same movies, but they still access the movies on the same platforms. Moving forward, organizers will need to see themselves as the platform that delivers great content to an array of niche audiences.

Like Nicola Kastner's innovative set design for SAPPHIRE 2019, the audience journey designed by event organizers should include freedom and flexibility for attendees to explore their own areas of interest through an easy-to-navigate platform. Like the experience found in content streaming and social media platforms, attendees should also be directed toward the content that best aligns with their interests, while being given the space and freedom to explore on their own.

Community

Part of what makes any experience worthwhile is sharing it with a like-minded community. We purchase movie, concert, and sporting event tickets to fill stiff seats and enjoy overpriced concessions not because we couldn't enjoy the same event at home, but because we as humans naturally enjoy shared experiences. One of the biggest limitations of virtual events today is their inability to facilitate strong community ties.

Moving forward, organizers will need to find new and innovative ways to build a sense of community across screens and

Internet connection lines. After all, sitting in an audience of 500 people feels more engaging with the knowledge that another 5,000 are watching at home. Watching the action from home similarly feels more engaging when you can see and feel the larger community around you.

One industry that has excelled at building communities around its content is the eSports industry. eSports tournaments pack stadiums with fans while broadcasting the events to thousands and even millions of at-home audience members. Those who have attended an eSports tournament know that fans help facilitate a festival-like atmosphere. In fact, many dress up in elaborate costumes for the occasion. That sense of community is clearly visible to both in-person and at-home audiences, who get to feel part of a larger community by attending eSports events.

eSports events provide a community that is typically widely dispersed. This was made abundantly clear during COVID-19, when the 2020 *League of Legends* World Championship, hosted in Shanghai, was held in a bubble in front of a limited audience, much like the NBA finals in the United States, discussed below (Dixon, 2020). The tournament matches were livestreamed throughout October, racking up a total of 139 million viewing hours from a worldwide audience— much to the delight of sponsors like Bose, Mercedes-Benz, Spotify, and Cisco (Fitch, 2020).

As the world of work becomes more remote and more decentralized, events will serve as a critical connection point for community engagement, as well as a continued goldmine for savvy sponsors looking to capture a new, passionate audience.

Experience Design

Experience design is the practice of designing products, services, events, omnichannel journeys, and environments with a focus on the quality and relevance of a user's experience. Taken together, each of the engagement principles we've reviewed so far culminate in an experience-first design that is a holistic and engaging experience for remote audiences.

As with most other aspects of today's consumer world, choice is not a luxury, but an expectation. Consumers—and audiences—expect the freedom to curate an experience that best suits their needs while simultaneously being "wowed" by unexpected surprises. They want to enjoy a personalized experience as well as a shared one with content that offers the value they actively seek as well as benefits they might not anticipate.

In-person audiences are often highly engaged in the experience because it's immersive, and in the coming years organizers will seek to extend that immersion to virtual attendees. Often the best way to create a more immersive experience for those attending remotely is by finding novel ways to bring them into the venue space.

One strong example of an organization that did this well during the pandemic is the NBA, which hosted a portion of its season in its bubble, closed off to in-person audiences. Understanding that fan engagement was important to both at-home audiences and the players themselves, the NBA displayed livestreams of virtual fans watching the game at home on screens that surrounded the court. As the season wore on, fans could be seen displaying their team colors, looking anxious in the final minutes of the game, and raising their arms in victory after a win. Eventually celebrities, basketball stars, even former president Barack Obama made an appearance at the games, without ever setting foot in the bubble itself.

The ability to interact with the in-person event as a remote attendee serves as an early example of what's to come in the hybrid events space. In-person audience members won't just be passive viewers; in the future they will be further engaged in the experience through direct interaction with the event venue space.

Accomplishing all of this in a virtual format is no easy feat, but the technology is quickly catching up. In the years ahead, we'll see significant innovation on each of these fronts, with each step further enabling experience-first design. In the meantime, however, organizers will need to get creative and consider ways to utilize the tools that are currently available.

Choosing the Right Format for the Right Outcome

Event leaders today are seeing their event strategies evolve from an exclusively in-person format to a digital-first format—where in-person events complement a larger virtual engagement strategy.

In this new environment each event format—in-person, virtual, and hybrid—presents a unique strategic application. Below is an overview of the advantages and disadvantages of each event format along with brief descriptions of where they are and are not effective, with a brief overview of best practices to keep in mind when designing an event experience for a specific format.

Virtual Events

Advantages

The primary advantage of virtual events is reach. As we discovered first-hand at the start of the pandemic with our (Almost) IN-PERSON event, the low barrier to entry allows event teams to reach a much broader audience on a virtual platform. It's similarly much easier to attract speakers and guests who would otherwise not fit in the event budget or be able to attend in person.

Other advantages include much greater data-capturing capabilities and thus greater insight into audience behaviors. As the technology improves, the expectation is that virtual events will be able to offer a content model that more closely resembles a content streaming service, where attendees are directed to the sessions that best suit their interests.

Virtual events are also typically less expensive to produce than in-person events and provide an opportunity for marketers to get creative. No longer limited by geographical constraints, virtual events can take viewers around the world, offering relevant information onsite from key locations.

Disadvantages

The most significant disadvantage that virtual event organizers will need to contend with is engagement. While attendees have the opportunity to participate in more events, they are also much less likely to dedicate significant time to each of them. Instead, attendees might log on to watch a handful of sessions that speak only to their interests or connect only with specific attendees. Sustaining attendee engagement thus remains a significant challenge.

Virtual events also need to contend with a world of distractions, ranging from emails and slack messages to at-home disruptions. Online events are also heavily reliant on the technology platforms that host them, as even a temporary service failure can derail an entire event.

Lastly, while technology is quickly catching up and the events industry may soon enjoy better ways to facilitate networking online, virtual events are simply unable to facilitate the type of deep relationship building that many expect from in-person experiences.

Best Used For

Virtual events are best used to cast a wide net and reach a broad audience. The relatively low cost and high reach make them perfect for engaging with audiences that wouldn't have otherwise attended in person. In marketing terms, they're ideal for brand awareness and more top-of-funnel activities.

Less Effective For

Virtual events still have limitations when it comes to facilitating a networking experience that matches that of in-person activations and as a result are less effective at driving community-building. Likewise, while virtual events can be huge for building interest in a product or service, they are less effective at driving bottom-of-the-funnel outcomes (like closing deals or expanding business with existing customers) where personal connection is critical. The inability to shake hands, make eye contact, or attend happy hours remains a significant challenge.

Best Practices

Keep it short In 2021 we conducted a study that validated the suspicions of many organizers: When it comes to virtual events, users generally prefer to consume content in bite-sized chunks. Specifically, we found that virtual attendees watch only 68 percent of sessions that last longer than 20 minutes, suggesting that engaging virtual audiences requires content that is both brief and highly relevant.

As a guiding principle, shorter virtual experiences are often better, both in terms of each individual session as well as the length of the event itself.

Unlock the power of data Virtual events offer a wide spectrum of data for organizers to capture, but the data's value can be realized only through effective utilization.

As Rexson Serrao from Salesforce put it: "What we weren't prepared for was this explosion of data because all of a sudden every system is capturing all of these logs, all of this plethora of data. We looked at one virtual event [and found] more data points than the entirety of our in-person portfolio last year."

To unlock the full potential of data, organizers need to offer audiences bespoke experiences based on the data they've provided about their interests and needs. For Rexson and his team, that means creating experiences that are "shorter" and "punchier." They are less about selling Salesforce and more about exploring how prospects and customers can be successful.

In-Person Events

Advantages

In-person events aren't going away anytime soon; however, they will be utilized in more purposeful ways moving forward. The key advantage of an in-person event is relationship-building. There really is no substitute for eye contact, handshakes, and in-person connection. In-person events are also more immersive and are naturally more effective at facilitating more engaging experiences.

With fewer distractions to contend with, in-person events will remain the best way to acquire an audience's undivided attention for prolonged periods. As on-demand event content becomes the norm, in-person-only events will be the only place for attendees to experience the intimacy, bonding, and level of relationship-building that they exclusively provide.

Disadvantages

The most significant disadvantages of in-person events are cost and complexity. In-person events are typically more expensive and logistically complicated than those that take place in a virtual space. They also require attendees and speakers to dedicate significant time and resources, which will serve to reduce the event's overall reach. That is especially true in the immediate future when business travel is expected to remain below pre-pandemic levels.

In the short term, organizers will also be challenged by ongoing health and safety requirements and travel restrictions. While virtual events rely heavily on technology, in-person events can be similarly derailed by extreme weather, flight cancellations, and traffic.

Best Used For

In-person events are best suited for facilitating more intimate and personal experiences. In marketing terms, they are ideal for more bottom-funnel activities, like closing deals or strengthening client relationships.

In-person events without any online component also have the opportunity to play on FOMO, or the "fear of missing out." In the future, we anticipate in-person events leaning into the exclusivity factor, emphasizing the importance of not missing out on a unique experience. In-person events are also more effective for presenting more complicated or longer-form content, such as product demonstrations, as they minimize (but do not completely eliminate) the distractions that attendees face when attending an event virtually.

In the long term, we anticipate that in-person events will once again be an effective touchpoint for uniting large in-person communities. In addition, as virtual events continue to move toward a choose-your-own-adventure model, we anticipate that in-person events will gradually absorb this same framework, resulting in experiences that are more personalized throughout the attendee's journey.

Less Effective For

In the short term, organizers will be hard-pressed to create large-scale in-person events similar to those we saw before the pandemic due in part to reduced budgets for business travel, health and safety concerns of attendees and sponsors, and tighter event-planning budgets. Live events are currently less effective at gathering attendee data that can be utilized to offer a more personalized event experience.

Best Practices

Be purposeful   Organizers have long defaulted to in-person events, but moving forward, in-person events should be used to achieve specific outcomes. If you cannot define why an event needs to be in-person rather than virtual or hybrid, you probably shouldn't be hosting an in-person event. The same goes for how you approach attendees, sponsors, and content; each should be considered within the context of the specific desired outcome.

Clearly communicate value   At least in the immediate future, audiences may be hesitant to attend in-person events and will likely have a harder time getting sign-off on business travel. As a result, organizers need to be very clear in their communications about why attendees should invest the time, effort, and resources to attend an event in person. Getting that rubber stamp from leadership will be a bigger challenge, so organizers need to see themselves as responsible for equipping prospective attendees with a sound argument that will help them get that approval.

Use exclusivity to your advantage   In-person events without a digital component exist only in a specific time and place before they're gone forever. While we often consider the ability to provide content on-demand to virtual audiences as an advantage, there is an added pull that comes from an event that can be experienced only in person. Organizers should lean into that element of exclusivity to increase interest and engagement at in-person events.

Keep it personal   While in-person events of the past could have attendee numbers in the tens of thousands, their advantage in the post-pandemic world will come from facilitating human connections, exclusivity, and immersion. Each of these advantages is at risk of being diluted with too many attendees vying for the same experiences or with the wrong experiences being offered to your attendees. Rather than casting a wide net, use in-person events to engage a specific audience for a specific purpose, such as introducing existing customers in a specific market to a new product or hosting an intimate retreat for chief marketing officers in a specific industry.

Think global, plan local   In the pre-pandemic era, it was common for attendees to travel from far and wide to attend events, but in the future, in-person events are likely to become more regional affairs. Rather than asking the audience to come to you, organizers will need to go to their audiences. Often that means hosting a series of smaller, more intimate events in a number of different regions, with content and speakers that reflect that specific market, rather than a one-size-fits-all global gathering.

Hybrid Events

Advantages

Hybrid events, by definition, offer an opportunity to combine the best of both in-person and virtual events. Because they exist across a spectrum, there are any number of ways that the two experiences can be combined.

Generally speaking, hybrid events allow organizers to cast a wide net that reaches the length of the Internet, while also offering a degree of intimacy and exclusivity to in-person guests. When executed properly, hybrid events have the potential to achieve a range of business outcomes simultaneously, across the entire sales funnel.

Disadvantages

The primary disadvantages of hybrid events are cost and complexity, as organizers are responsible for engaging two distinct audiences in two different mediums, while simultaneously bridging the divide between them.

While hybrid events offer the opportunity to achieve a range of business outcomes when executed well, they also have the potential to fail on multiple fronts at the same time. Hybrid events are also less likely to provide the cost advantages of online-only events, and they lack the exclusivity of in-person-only events.

Best Used For

Hybrid events offer an opportunity to engage a vast virtual audience while offering high levels of engagement for in-person attendees. They also offer attendees more flexibility and the opportunity to attend the event in whatever format best suits them.

Hybrid events are best used to achieve the outcomes that large-scale flagship events provided in the past, including brand and community building, networking, relationship building, education, and lead acquisition.

Less Effective For

While hybrid events offer many of the advantages of both in-person and virtual events, there are still some limitations. For example, having a virtual audience can increase reach but reduce the level of intimacy and exclusivity for in-person attendees.

At the same time, hybrid events need to balance the need for providing a high-quality production for virtual audiences without sacrificing the in-person experience. As a result, hybrid event producers will be more limited in the type of content they can produce as compared with virtual-only events.

Best Practices

Find ways to connect in-person and virtual attendees
Hybrid events will always be at risk of feeling like two distinct engagements. In order to realize the community-building potential of hybrid events, however, organizers will have to find ways to bridge the gap between the two.

In some cases that could mean facilitating hybrid networking sessions, or hybrid panels, or finding creative ways for digital attendees to influence and engage with the in-person environment. In the coming years, we expect technology to help bridge the gap, but in the meantime, organizers will need to come up with some creative solutions of their own.

Offer two unique attendee experiences In a hybrid environment, it's important that neither audience feels left out of the experience. While it's important to offer connection points between virtual and in-person attendees, it's also important to use the advantages provided by each to offer an experience that is somewhat unique to that medium. That could mean a more data-driven approach and a streaming platform-like recommendation engine for virtual attendees, as well as more intimate and exclusive events for in-person attendees, like post-event happy hour networking sessions. What's important is that neither audience feels like an afterthought compared to the other.

Enable attendees to move seamlessly between in-person and online While we often think of hybrid audiences as being "either-or," it's important not to forget the audience members who will choose "both." In some cases, attendees may want to attend one day of an event in person and two more online, and organizers need to be prepared to offer them that degree of freedom and flexibility. When designing hybrid events, it's important to consider how you will enable some audience members to choose both, rather than one or the other.

CHAPTER
11

Content

As we have made clear, content is the key to engagement. Until technology enables virtual networking that is on par with in-person networking, content will remain the primary driver of virtual attendance.

According to a series of studies we conducted in the spring of 2021, nearly half of virtual attendees logged into events because they were "very interested" in learning, and another 20 percent did so for the sole purpose of learning. As we stated earlier, virtual attendees watch only 68 percent of sessions that last longer than 20 minutes and on average around 50 percent of any given virtual session, suggesting that engaging virtual audiences requires content that is both brief and highly relevant.

While the amount of time attendees spend at each virtual event is less than what they would typically dedicate to an in-person engagement, our research found that they also attend a larger number of events overall. That same study found that almost 46 percent of respondents had attended 10 or more online events in the previous 12 months. By comparison, less than 13 percent attended 10 or more in-person events the year prior.

The picture that's emerging is one of choice and personalization. Attendees will register for a larger number of events but are likely to engage only with the content that's directly relevant to their needs and interests. While the number of attendees at virtual events will increase, the number of sessions they participate in will significantly decline.

As events evolve from in-person to virtual and hybrid engagements, organizers will be challenged to use data to deliver content that offers each attendee valuable and relevant information, based on their specific needs.

Virtual Attendee Personas

Through research we conducted in February 2021, we concluded that there are six unique personality types that attend events, each for their own reasons. Below is a list of each persona category, the persona type, and the goals of each one.

Management
Learning

- Mandated Learner: Learning/little internal networking
- Solo Learner: Learning/almost no networking

Networking

- Internal Socializer: Internal networking/little learning
- Radical Networker: Human connection/some learning
- Strategic Networker: Business networking/no learning

Fun

- Experience Seeker: No networking/some learning

The most prominent of these six personas in the virtual space was what we dubbed the *Solo Learner*. According to our research, this personality type accounts for 32 percent of online event attendees, but only 11 percent of in-person attendees.

The Solo Learners out there typically register for multiple free or inexpensive virtual events every week, even committing to multiple events on the same day. They don't always make an appearance at each event, but when they do log on, they are squarely focused on learning about their industry or role.

The second most prominent virtual attendee type is what we call the *Mandated Learner*, who is required to attend events for professional development purposes. This segment makes up 25 percent of virtual attendees and 26 percent of in-person audience members. However, unlike the Solo Learner, who is self-motivated, the Mandated Learner isn't necessarily there by choice and may have a harder time navigating online platforms.

The other four personas, each accounting for 18 percent of virtual attendees or less, were much more focused on networking and experience and were more likely to prioritize in-person attendance in the future.

Consequently, organizers should keep Solo Learners and Mandated Learners top of mind as they consider who will be consuming their content online, and why.

These personas can also help guide the development of segmented session tracks, email campaigns, and in-person activities. After all, attracting the Mandated Learner type to an event requires a different strategy than one used to attract Solo Learners. Knowing what your virtual attendees want from the experience, and how engaged they are likely to be with the content, can help you create experiences that meet their needs.

Breaking Through the Noise with Personalization

To stand out in a more heavily crowded playing field, organizers will need to focus on delivering and curating high-quality content directly to virtual attendees. Breaking through the noise will require matching attendees with their preferred content types and topics and delivering quality rather than overwhelming attendees with quantity.

As the number of online event opportunities increases, attendees will be less likely to spend hours digging through speaker lists and content schedules to find the sessions that meet those needs. According to IBM's vice president of conferences and events, Colleen Bisconti, big data and AI will be instrumental in matching the right person with the right content at the right time:

> All of a sudden I don't need to look through all the events that I'm invited to, which by the way is like a gazillion a day. I don't need to look, if this event is interesting to me, what should I do? All of a sudden I have this assistant that's helping me navigate based on my interests, and what they know about me, and now I'm crafting this very personalized experience. I don't have to worry about looking through laundry lists and pages of agenda topics. I don't have to search; it's just "Here you go." I'd be much more apt to go to an event and stay at an event if it was more personalized to me, and that's where I think we're headed.

Colleen explains that at the start of the pandemic she and her team thought the relatively low cost of virtual events would allow IBM to offer more content, but her thinking around content has since changed. "It allowed us to create more noise, because it was easier to put it into market, but just because you can do more events doesn't mean you should," she said.

In the lead up to Think 2021, IBM's annual flagship event, Colleen says she and her team focused on segmenting audiences based on roles, industries, and whether they would be interested in business-level activities or technical education. In an age where virtual events are abundant and are relatively cheap and easy to access for attendees in comparison to in-person events, virtual event content will need to be delivered in a more personalized manner—one that meets the needs of each individual attendee.

As Joey Graziano, the senior vice president of business operations and global events for the NBA, shared with us on the IN-PERSON Podcast: "We have to constantly look at the lack of tailored experiences that will lead our fans or our customers to choose an alternate environment. We have to embrace that everything that we do has to be custom curated for particular audiences at our events."

Adding Production Value

At the start of the pandemic, many online events featured speakers talking directly into their computer cameras at home. As health and safety restrictions eased, organizations were able to utilize more professional studio spaces and equipment.

Colleen Bisconti says even minor video quality improvements went a long way in increasing engagement. "The content that was better produced, meaning I had certain content that was captured in a studio, or somebody in their home that was standing—this is going to sound so silly, but standing instead of sitting in front of a bookcase—that content was consumed longer on average than other content [that paid less attention to production]," she says. "So as important as the content itself is, the production quality matters."

Bringing Audiences into the Conversation

Experience is just as important as content. Virtual attendees will always be at risk of feeling removed from the content, which is why it's important to find ways to bring them into the conversation directly.

When content is presented live onstage, audiences naturally feel like they are able to contribute directly to what's being presented, even through simple reactions like clapping, laughing, or just showing up and filling a seat. When content is delivered online, there is often a disconnect between presenters and audiences, with each feeling isolated from the other.

Allowing virtual attendees the opportunity to pose questions and engage in live audience polling is a good start, but moving forward organizers will need to find more creative ways of bringing audiences into the conversation.

Mark Wilson, the executive creative director of the event and content marketing agency Cramer, illustrated the importance of interactivity during a panel at our (Almost) Hybrid event in November 2020. He explained that there are big, flashy, expensive ways to draw virtual audiences into the live event experience, as well as some simpler, lower-tech solutions that can make a big impact:

> I like this word "presence," and I think it's going to become more a part of our vocabulary as we're designing and planning programs. How are you creating a real presence for your virtual audience in your venue space? I love the NBA [bubble] example, and there's a lot of examples of how people are doing it. It's the presence and then it's creating those interaction elements, trying to create more of a borderless experience. . . . Even in a general session there are ways to keep it interactive. I saw a presentation the other day where a presenter was using the chat function almost like it was a live radio show. He would ask a question of the audience and they would answer in the chat, and he would weave their answers into his monologue, and it was really effective. . . . That's really simple, but simple tools can also connect us in addition to the big fun things we do.

This transition toward interactive content was already underway prior to the pandemic but became even more vital in a virtual setting.

"For the longest time we said, 'Show me; don't tell me,' so we tried to create environments that were about showing, not telling," says Colleen Bisconti. "Then we moved to, 'Let me experience it,' so don't just show me, but let me touch and feel and experience what you mean by that. What we were moving to was 'Let me experience it my way,' and that same structure is in its infancy across digital. We've moved away from broadcast and watch—even though there are still times where broadcast and watch has value—and we've moved toward interactiveness."

Using the Medium to Complement the Message

When moving pictures were first sold to audiences at the turn of the nineteenth century, the industry's first instinct was to take what it already knew and adapt it to the big screen. That is why the first films were actually just recordings of stage plays, shot from a stationary camera in the audience. New technology doesn't erase old habits, and there's historical proof that our first instinct with something new is to recreate the old. It often takes years for people with fresh eyes to utilize the strengths of an emerging medium to their fullest.

Like the early film industry, we are very much in the experimental phase of virtual event content. Rather than broadcasting what would otherwise be said on stage—sometimes referred to as a "lift and shift" strategy—organizers should consider ways to utilize the unique advantages this new medium can offer and develop content that is native to the platform.

"What digital-first gives us is the realization that there are types of content that can be consumed digitally, the same way or better, as they can face-to-face," explained Colleen Bisconti. As the pandemic wore on, she says she and her team focused more on delivering virtual content that wouldn't be possible in an in-person setting. "Instead of just showcasing our client stories through people on stage talking about them, what if we go stand on a wind turbine? Or get on an oil rig? I wanted to have this feeling of a live broadcast," she says.

Moving forward, virtual content will likely comprise a mix of live broadcasting, prerecorded short films, interactive elements, and other storytelling techniques that haven't yet been developed. Immersive experiences—using virtual and augmented reality—could also have a significant impact on the way event content is packaged and delivered in the years ahead. What's important is that organizers aren't simply taking content from one medium and transplanting it to another. Instead, organizers should consider the unique features of each medium and design content around those features.

Extending the Value of Content Through On-Demand Services

In recent years organizers have found ways to increase the value of their events by offering content on-demand. In fact, a study we conducted in 2021 found that 80 percent of organizers who produce virtual event programs enable the capability for content to be accessed on-demand. Moving forward, we see the second life of content driving even greater value for attendees, both in person and virtual.

As with the content itself, the full value of these sessions can be realized only through personalization and recommendation engines. Users are unlikely to spend hours digging through clips to find the sessions that will provide value, but organizers can increase the value of their content by serving it to the right audience members at the right time.

This is one of the ways we envision digital events moving toward more of a Netflix-like content-streaming platform model. In the future, attendees will register for events to gain access to the library of content it produces, even if they are unable to join a single session as it is being broadcasted. The trend is in line with the growing demand for more personalization as well as more flexibility, because on-demand content can be consumed anywhere and anytime.

On-demand content effectively extends the duration of the event well beyond the days it actually took place. It also provides a valuable tool organizers can use to engage with prospects, attendees, and clients. Just as Netflix offers content "because you watched X," event producers can use this library of on-demand content to make recommendations based on the attendee's previous viewing patterns.

Furthermore, on-demand content can serve as a marketing tool for future events. Organizers can point potential attendees to a speaker's session from the previous year to entice them into registering for that speaker's next talk. As we move into the hybrid era, on-demand content will allow event sessions to provide value that extends well beyond the boundaries of the event itself. It will also be instrumental in building communities based on shared interests and experiences.

Community

Humans are social creatures by nature; we crave the sense of belonging that can come only from feeling part of a community.

Community building has always been a mainstay of event strategy. Events have long been one of the most valuable community-building tools in the broader marketing portfolio. While in-person interaction was previously the key to building that community, we as an industry have taken significant strides in a relatively short period of time when it comes to online community building. Much of that progress has come from combining the event-based community-building strategies organizers are already well accustomed to with the virtual community-building strategies borrowed from other industries.

With virtual event platforms dramatically extending the reach of events, there is now an opportunity to attract and develop a much broader community. At the same time, organizers will be challenged by the need to keep those communities vibrant and valuable beyond the length of the event itself.

"The whole community thing isn't new; for many years publishers have tried to form communities of professionals who interact not just at live events, but in the months that precede and follow the event," explained the *Financial Times* managing director of FT Live events, Orson Francescone. "The Holy Grail has always been a 12-month marketing cycle, where people interact on the community platform and meet once a year face-to-face, and it's never really worked very well, because you kind of need a big network effect for that to work."

In other words, event platforms never had the critical mass required to carry a community through the extended periods between events. The move to online platforms, the increased frequency of events enabled by low-cost virtual programs, and the extended reach of online events may finally lead organizers to that Holy Grail.

Building Community Through Virtual Events

According to Orson Francescone, organizers who tried to engage those communities in the periods between events often felt like they were showing up to an empty ballroom.

"How you curate those communities apart from the event days has always been a difficult challenge, but we're quite well placed to try that out," he says. "We are going to experiment with bringing communities around big industry verticals together with an offering that has obviously our content, our journalism, our special reports, our events, making new networking events, maybe an interactive networking platform, so we are curating a digital community platform."

Rather than feeling like they've shown up to an empty ballroom, Orson says community members need to feel like they are exploring a primary resource of industry knowledge. If individuals log on to see respected members of their professional community engaging with the platform, they are more likely to follow along and engage with it too.

Fortunately, event teams are well positioned to become the facilitators of these online communities. And in the virtual age, that community has the potential to provide significant value to organizers who can pull it off effectively.

Prior to the pandemic, the *Financial Times* hosted roughly 200 events each year, ranging from breakfast briefings to two-day conferences, with the largest events hosting around 600 attendees, according to Orson Francescone. When the pandemic hit, he says that he and his team, like many in the events industry, suddenly found themselves in the midst of an existential crisis, unsure of whether their business would survive. In the first week of April 2020, only weeks after the first lockdown measures were put into place, FT ran what it called the "Global Economic Emergency" conference. The one-hour webinar featured a number of high-profile economists discussing the financial implications of the pandemic.

"We launched this webinar on the Monday, and we ran it on the Friday, so we had five days to market the event, and we ended up with 6,000 registrations, which was a real revelation for us, because we're used to, I'd say our average event attendees [number] around the 300 to 400 mark," explained Orson.

FT Live followed up the webinar five weeks later with an event called "Global Boardroom," bringing together 120 policymakers and economists from all over the world. Speakers included former Prime Minister Tony Blair, governors of the Central Bank of England and the Federal Reserve, the chairman of the IMF, and CEOs from a range of major global organizations. "If you were to put that kind of event together in the physical world it would probably take you two years," he says. "We did it in five weeks, which was incredible."

The event was free for attendees and monetized through sponsorships. On the opening day, Global Boardroom had 25,000 registrants from around the world. By the end of the event three days later, there were almost 52,000. "That was a huge moment for the FT, because we were the first big media event organizer to pull off something of that size and scale," says Orson.

The primary driver of the event's success, according to Orson, was its ability to reach audiences that had never attended an FT event before. "In a normal pre-COVID year, FT Live would convene about 25,000 delegates across all our events; last year we ended up with more than 280,000 registrations at our events, more than a tenfold increase in registrations, which is mind blowing," he says. "For a business like the FT, where the subscriptions to our magazine is the main revenue driver, bringing in new data has a huge amount of value, because those new delegates can be upsold into a subscription. But it gives you the idea of the scale of the transformation."

Orson says he soon realized that the future of events for FT Live would no longer look like 300 high-profile attendees in a Four Seasons ballroom in London. He was now in the community-building business. "We're very much now a digital-first business, is what I tell the team. We will go back to live events, but we'll go back only if and when it makes sense," he says.

Digital-first forever is the phrase I use, and of course we'll go back to physical events, but they will always have a digital component, because we don't want to lose those big global audiences. Digitization has allowed us to evangelize and prophesize the FT word across every corner for the globe, from Japan to Latin America, and we're reaching audiences that we would have never reached before. A lot of these people, it's not like they would come to our in-person events. We had people in Chile and Tasmania watching our events; those aren't former physical event attendees that are watching at home; those are completely new people we would never have reached before. We don't want to lose hold of those new engaged global audiences, and the only way of doing that is maintaining a digital-first approach to our events, even when we return to physical events.

Orson's experience demonstrates how event organizers are naturally inclined to bring together large communities of like-minded people, especially on digital platforms that drastically reduce the barrier to entry. Reaching critical mass remains the most significant challenge of building a vibrant community.

Taking a Seat at the Marketing Table

According to Colleen Bisconti, effective community building in the virtual era will require further integration with broader marketing efforts. She explains that events have long been seen as a standalone marketing activity, one that served to solve specific marketing needs, but not always integrated into high-level strategy. "I don't think that events have blurred into marketing; events have integrated into the end-to-end marketing journey," she says.

> I think where event marketers struggled was it was a one-off, or we have a gap in our pipeline, or we're challenged in this country, "let's throw some events at it; that will fix it," instead of really understanding where those event touch points—now digital first, physical with purpose—fit into those marketing campaigns, or campaign journeys. Whatever you call them, this will give us a chance to better integrate, versus being these single-point touch points that happen where you hope people connect to other things that are happening.

Colleen believes that moving forward, event organizers will need to have a seat at the table when it comes to broader campaign and go-to-market strategy. Doing so will effectively allow them to evolve from a temporary multiday community to a year-round gathering, and one that is directly aligned to business outcomes.

Offering Can't-Miss Shared Experiences

We naturally crave a sense of belonging within our personal and professional communities, which is why community development is often driven by our emotions. It's not enough to entice members with a discount to the next event or some other perk for signing up and engaging with a community. Members need to feel an emotional connection to their fellow members. This tends to happen naturally once a community reaches critical mass, but when it comes to building a foundation, nothing beats a shared emotional experience. Fortunately, event organizers are well practiced at offering those can't-miss moments that often drive community engagement.

The pandemic period was a particularly interesting time to be in the community-building business. On the one hand, newly isolated and widely dispersed community members craved human connection and the ability to share their experiences with others in their industry. On the other hand, much of the technology that helps facilitate those communities lives in the corners of large social networks, like Reddit forums, LinkedIn communities, Facebook groups, and Twitter hashtags.

Moving those industry-based communities onto virtual event platforms will require both the functionality and ease of use offered by those social network platforms and industry forums, coupled with exclusive content and shared experiences that cannot be attained elsewhere. As organizers consider ways to bring communities onto their platforms, it's important to offer those can't-miss experiences that only exist on their platforms. That could be a Q&A session with industry leaders, exclusive events and content, giveaways, competitions that lean on gamification strategies, and more.

Today, Reddit is the 7th most-visited website in the United States, and 19th in the world, but for much of its early history, the online forum was considered a niche social media platform that served specific online communities (Alexa, 2021). Then in 2012 the platform offered its users something none of its competitors could, catapulting the website to the top of the Internet's most popular websites. That unannounced surprise event gave users the opportunity to ask Barack Obama anything they wanted, and the sitting president responded to a range of questions posed by users. That day in August 2012 marked Reddit's biggest day in terms of user engagement and effectively cemented it as a platform that provided its community something none of its competitors could (Jeffries, 2012).

Communities are built on individual members, but the opportunity to engage with otherwise inaccessible community leaders is what often brings those members together. As organizers seek to build virtual communities, they should consider ways to offer their users shared emotional experiences that would be otherwise unattainable. Offering those moments unannounced is also an effective way of keeping them engaged, waiting for the next big surprise.

CHAPTER

13

Experience Design

The event organizer's job has always centered on attendee experience, and that will remain the industry's North Star moving forward, even as we change platforms and experiment with new technologies. In fact, much of the innovation we're anticipating—and to some extent, are already seeing—in the events space is focused on improving the attendee experience as part of the larger movement around experience-first design.

Providing a quality experience in an in-person-only format was already enough of a challenge. As organizers know, experience isn't just one thing, but the sum of many parts. Those parts can range from the event content to layout and design, networking opportunities, registration and check-in, and even the venue itself.

Experience encompasses an attendee's first moments clicking through to an event website, their first moments stepping in the virtual or in-person venue, and the way that the content and community facilitated by the event continue to serve as a touch point for attendees after the event concludes. In a virtual context, many of those real-world experiential design elements need to be transported into a digital platform or be replaced with an alternative that better suits the medium.

In the years ahead, event planners will have their work cut out for them, because providing a memorable experience will only become more challenging on a computer, tablet, or phone screen. Furthermore, organizers will need to continue providing a stellar in-person experience, as well as a memorable online experience, while simultaneously finding ways to facilitate a shared experience between the two.

Designing Experiences That Attendees Actually Want

We previously outlined some of the research we conducted in early 2021 that found six distinct event attendee personas, focusing on the two most common virtual attendees: the Solo Learner and the Mandated Learner. While those two personality types were squarely focused on education, the other four had different priorities when attending events.

The Radical Networker, for example, is all about making connections. Representing 18 percent of virtual and 15 percent of in-person attendees, this personality type is all about the social aspects of events. Their top reason for attending events is making new friends, and their second priority is increasing their networks.

The Strategic Networker, by comparison, isn't looking to increase the quantity of their connections, but the quality. Comprising 17 percent of in-person attendees and only 10 percent of online attendees, this personality type sees networking as a vital part of their job.

The Internal Socializer, meanwhile, attends events to engage and have fun with friends and colleagues and is less interested in attending sessions. Comprising only 8 percent of virtual attendees and a whopping 25 percent of all in-person attendees, this personality type sees events as a key opportunity to strengthen relationships with colleagues and team members.

And finally, the Experience Seeker loves to have a good time at events. Comprising 12 percent of in-person attendees and only 7 percent of online attendees, this personality type loves gifts and giveaways, travel, dinners with friends, and after-hours experiences. They attend for the wow factor, the swag, and the excitement that comes from traveling to a large event.

While the Learners are more likely to prioritize virtual events moving forward, these four personality types will find more of what they're looking for by attending events in person.

As organizers begin to plot their hybrid event strategies, it's important to keep all six of these unique personality types in mind and consider who will likely arrive in person and who will tune in remotely. While it's important to offer both online and in-person audiences all of the benefits that come with event attendance, it's also important to understand your audiences' priorities and cater to their needs.

Organizers should therefore work to ensure that each personality type is able to get what they're looking for out of their events, while prioritizing educational opportunities for online attendees and experiences for in-person audiences.

Personalizing the Experience

Key to a strong user experience is providing a strong degree of personalization. Streaming platforms like Netflix, social media platforms like Facebook and Twitter, and online retail giants like Amazon aren't successful only because of the quantity of content and products they offer; their real value is in how their products and services are delivered to the user.

What separates today's most successful technology platforms and products from their competitors often comes down to ease of use and personalization. When you log onto Netflix, you're offered recommendations that speak to your unique interests. When you log onto Amazon, the front page offers a list of items you are likely to purchase. When you sign onto a social media platform, your feed is populated by content that you are most likely to engage with.

The same will be increasingly true within the events space. Having a gigantic library of content is only as valuable as the ability to navigate easily to the sessions that offer real value to the individual user. The same is true for networking, where quality will often trump quantity in terms of creating a positive user experience. Having the data and tools to deliver a personalized experience is vital for event success, no matter the format.

Designing Experiences Based on Outcomes

Understanding why different types of people attend events, coupled with data and tools that can help offer a more personalized experience, will allow the industry to move toward a strategy of outcome-based design. Rather than offering attendees an overwhelming array of sessions to attend and people to meet and asking them to curate their own experiences, we as an industry need to put the desired outcome first and work our way backwards. Outcome-based design requires a strong understanding of what attendees want to achieve and then designing experiences that will allow them to achieve it.

Focusing on User Experience

Those in the technology industry are well accustomed to speaking about products and services in terms of user experience, or UX, and now is the time for event teams to adopt the term. User experience design, like event experience, encompasses a wide range of factors, from the ease of finding important information at a glance to the speed at which web pages and online tools load. All of these elements, no matter how small, build an overall user experience that can make technology products either difficult to use or difficult to put down.

The same is true in the events space. No matter how strong the content, networking, and other elements of the event are, the whole event will fall flat without a strong focus on user experience. After all, if you attend an otherwise flawless event but have to wait in line several hours each day, or if the food is unbearable, or if there aren't enough bathrooms, you'll probably remember that event in negative terms.

The same is true of online platforms. If users need to dedicate a lot of time and effort to enjoy your content, they probably won't have a positive experience, no matter how strong that content is. As events integrate more technology, it's important to maintain a strong focus on user experience design, among both in-person and remote attendees.

Sharing the Experience

Part of what makes the event experience so memorable and magical is sharing it with others. Shared experiences give us a sense of being part of something bigger than ourselves, and events have long been the perfect venue for those moments.

As many discovered in the immediate aftermath of the transition to virtual events, replicating that sense of community and shared experience is far more complicated in a virtual setting. As we move toward a more hybrid future, it will be incumbent on organizers to offer that sense of a shared experience, even for those attending alone from home.

This is where the integration of virtual and in-person attendees becomes vital. Feeling the presence of virtual attendees in the physical venue, and vice-versa, can help elevate the event experience for both audiences. As discussed earlier, there are a variety of ways to facilitate that interactivity between audiences. Some examples include displaying a livestream of virtual attendees at the event venue (as was done in the NBA bubble), allowing virtual attendees to ask questions directly to speakers on stage, and providing virtual attendees with tools that allow them to applaud or engage in real time.

This is another area where live content holds a strong advantage over prerecorded content, and why organizers should strive to encourage virtual attendees to watch sessions live, even if they are available on demand at a later date. As technology enables virtual attendees to have their presence felt in the venue spaces, it's important for organizers to give them a reason to attend live, rather than watching the content later on demand. After all, it's not really a shared experience if a large proportion of the audience doesn't show up until days later.

Harnessing the Wow Factor

In-person events have long been a venue for experiences that are largely unattainable elsewhere, from an intimate concert to a surprise celebrity appearance to giveaways and product demos. As we move toward more virtual and hybrid events, it's important not to forget to integrate elements of surprise and delight—in other words, the wow factor. In some cases, organizers will find that those moments of surprise and wonder translate easily into a digital format, but in many cases, organizers will need to get creative.

Fortunately, many of the same principles of wowing an in-person audience still apply to those attending virtually. Gamification, contests, prizes, awards, and giveaways are still effective ways to facilitate a positive event experience, even in a virtual setting. Some of the more creative examples we've seen recently include scavenger hunts that award virtual attendees for finding items around their own homes and displaying them on camera, gaming events that allowed users to try an early copy of an unreleased game, and gifts and swag delivered directly to attendees' doors.

A strong example of incorporating the wow factor into an event is the 2020 Emmy Awards. Prior to the remote award ceremony, ABC shipped a black box to each nominee in a number of select categories. During the ceremony, nominees had their boxes on hand, and when the winner was announced, their box burst open to reveal the award statue inside. Fellow nominees, meanwhile, opened their boxes to find a consolation bottle of champagne (which had the strategic benefit of being approximately the same size and weight as the award itself).

Despite being filmed remotely, the event still managed to pull off a wow factor that surprised and delighted. The boxes themselves served as a source of mystery and anticipation, and the reveal during the award show facilitated the surprise and delight viewers were expecting.

Humanizing Virtual and Hybrid Events Through Technology

We've come a long way in just over a year of facilitating virtual event experiences, but it's important to remember that event technology is still in its infancy, relatively speaking. In the years ahead, the virtual venue space will be reinvented and improved upon in ways we can't even begin to predict today. The pace of innovation will come at breakneck speeds as new solutions begin to enter the market. Many of these new innovations will help to humanize the virtual event experience, likely through enhanced personalization, better remote networking, and more opportunities for virtual audiences to engage with those attending in person. Providing a strong event experience requires a strong understanding of—and a certain degree of comfort using—the tools that are made available. It's an exciting time to be in the events industry, but only for those who are ready to embrace rapid change and innovation.

Our goal as an industry is to ensure everyone feels like they're part of a community and can share in the emotions of others. Those shared experiences at events will be reinvented in many ways in the coming years, with new tools to amplify those emotional layers. Utilizing those tools to their fullest potential will require event professionals to adopt new skills and capabilities, but the transition will also enable them to become much more central to their organization's sales and marketing strategies.

PART

IV

People and Process

CHAPTER

14

The Rise of the Event Experience Manager

The events industry is rapidly transforming itself to focus on outcomes and experience. Aided by new ways of analyzing data, the events of 2020 and 2021 clarified the need for planners to focus on outcomes. And while events have long been about experiences, the evolution of the experience economy and its focus on customer success have sharpened the need for planners to concentrate on the experiences of their attendees, partners, and team members. To thrive in this emerging landscape will require new skills, new teams, and new names for the work that event planners carry out.

In the past, *event planners* was a term synonymous with *event managers*. As the titles imply, the job primarily focused on logistics, such as venue contracts, catering, travel, budgeting, and other practical concerns related to hosting a large gathering. Moving forward, event professionals will need to demonstrate these same skills along with a range of new capabilities. Instead of building a venue and a physical activation, their role will be to design experiences across the attendee journey—experiences that exist in both physical and virtual worlds.

As far back as 2016, Sherrif Karamat, the CEO of the Professional Convention Management Association (PCMA)—the world's largest network of event professionals—proposed a new title for event professionals, suggesting it was a better reflection of emerging requirements and expectations within the industry. The following year, PCMA outlined the need for *event planners* to evolve into *event strategists*, adopting a new title that would better suit their role.

PCMA has since dropped the words *planner* and *organizer* from its vocabulary and now offers courses and content specific to event *strategists*. While many forward-looking organizations have since adopted the new title, the transition taking place in the industry has ultimately demonstrated the need for event professionals and their colleagues to think of themselves as more than planners or organizers or even coordinators.

That's not only because some event professionals may no longer coordinate and plan physical events, despite having an otherwise active events portfolio. The title change also speaks to the point along the journey event where professionals are called in to lend their expertise. In the modern context, event professionals are no longer employed to coordinate or plan how to bring someone else's vision to life. Event professionals are now a key resource much earlier in the process, helping other stakeholders solve real business needs through a strong event strategy. Calling them event *planners*, despite their involvement in high-level strategy, no longer does their efforts justice.

We generally agree with this viewpoint but raise it a step further. In the future, organizations will seek to empower event professionals to design and manage experiences that are anchored in tangible business outcomes. This transition will ultimately be reflected in a new title, moving away from the previous responsibility of "planning" or "organizing" an event, toward one tied to "experience." This is the age of the **event experience manager**.

Making the Transition

Making the leap from event planner to event experience manager requires more than a simple title change. By definition, event experience managers are responsible for creating an attendee experience that directly corresponds to business needs, utilizing all the necessary available tools to get the job done. The unfortunate reality is that strategy was never the primary focus of the industry, and many of its members were never trained as such.

Event experience requires a different set of skills than event organizing, even though organizing is still a key attribute of strategy. That sentiment was also echoed by a number of other thought leaders within the industry.

"For anybody who views themselves as an event marketer, or a face-to-face experiential person, this has been particularly difficult, because not only have our lives changed, but our jobs changed," says Colleen Bisconti, vice president of conferences and events for IBM.

"This is an event team that is used to running events in five-star hotels, and suddenly they need to run digital conferences on a platform they've never used before," adds Orson Francescone, the managing director of FT Live.

"The muscle that events people really need to develop more is being more strategic in the approach of the event, and really thinking about what's the currency of this thing, and what are we trying to achieve?" says Dana Pake, an events industry thought leader who has led event programs at companies like GitHub, InVision, and Tableau.

The Event Experience Leaders of the Future

The shift to virtual events in 2021 saw the rise of the executive event producer: someone with the broadcasting and production know-how to captivate audiences through the medium of the screen. With virtual, in-person, and hybrid formats on the table, event experience managers will need to demonstrate a range of skills in order to realize the full value of their events portfolio. Those skills include the traditional event planning and organizing skills of the past, coupled with some baseline understanding of data and how it can be used to achieve business outcomes.

Event experience managers should also have some degree of comfort with the technology tools that will support those efforts, a strong understanding of marketing and sales functions more broadly, and the role that events play in the broader marketing portfolio.

They will also need to demonstrate a range of softer skills that are too often overlooked but are of even greater importance in today's events landscape. Event professionals have long held one of the most stressful jobs in the enterprise, but hybrid events only add another layer of complexity, making attributes like resilience, grit, and remaining calm under pressure even more necessary. Event experience managers will also need to showcase strong communication skills, empathy and understanding, collaboration, and creative problem solving in order to thrive in a hybrid ecosystem.

As you consider what it will take to thrive in this new world of virtual and hybrid events, it's important to consider the hard skills many associate with this transition—namely, technology, data, and marketing strategy—alongside the more behavioral skills that will be critical in navigating this quickly changing landscape.

As event experience managers are required to wear more hats and work with a wider array of cross-functional teams, the industry will also increasingly come to value a broad range of relevant experiences as highly as those with a significant degree of expertise in a single area.

For example, if the ideal candidate of the past had a master's degree in event management, the ideal candidate of the future might have majored in psychology and earned a minor in computer science with an event planning certificate. As event teams are tasked with borrowing solutions from other domains and working more closely with different teams and departments, the industry will increasingly see the value in enriching their teams with professionals from nontraditional backgrounds.

Building Diverse and Inclusive Teams

Just as a diversity of skills and expertise will prove advantageous to event teams of the future, so too will a diversity of cultures and communities. With remote and hybrid events enabling far greater reach, strategists will be increasingly challenged to serve audiences outside of their geographical region, making diversity and inclusion a key consideration for event professionals and teams of the future. Events have long been an opportunity to showcase diverse opinions and perspectives, but the switch to virtual events only furthers the importance of inclusivity.

Take Orson Francescone, for example. As the managing director at FT Live, Orson was accustomed to hosting intimate events for a few hundred London-based economists and thought leaders. Orson is now catering to a global audience of more than 280,000 registrants from every corner of the planet. Whereas diversity and inclusion have long been considered a matter of corporate social responsibility, understanding the unique needs and cultural sensitivities of such a diverse audience is no longer a feel-good exercise, but a business imperative.

That imperative extends from the makeup of the event team itself to the attendees, presenters, and panelists. With audience members of all shapes and sizes tuning into your event from anywhere in the world, and with engagement top of mind, it's important for every audience member to see their own experiences reflected back at them.

As Dana Pake explains, events are all about building a community, and in the virtual world that community transcends traditional borders and boundaries. "Events are about people, and when people feel seen, heard, understood, and feel like they belong, that translates into affinity, and affinity will then turn into dollars," she says. "If I feel like I belong and I feel connected and I feel like my voice is not only represented but included and heard, I might even forgive that your product missed its ship [date] or a feature didn't deliver what was promised, because you created a space for me to belong and connect with like-minded people at your program."

For a long time, diversity and inclusion meant ensuring equal gender representation among speakers, and while it's important to ensure women are equally represented on stage, that's only just the beginning, advises Andrea Long, the former global diversity events manager for Twilio. "We also have to think about women who are people with disabilities as well, or women who are of different minority groups, or women who are veterans," she says. "How are we making sure that we're looking at people not just in sort of this one-minded binary way, and also considering how we can diversify not just our speakers but our attendees? How are we outreaching to different audiences to make sure that if our speakers are a diverse set of people, our attendees also are? I think there's a lot of opportunities in this area, specifically in events."

Elevating the Role of Event Professionals

Changing job requirements, descriptions, and even titles can be an intimidating prospect, but the transition from planner to event experience manager will ultimately serve to elevate the role of events and event professionals within the organization's broader marketing portfolio. No longer just in charge of logistics and planning, event professionals will be tasked with aligning their activations, both in-person and virtual, with business goals and marketing strategies. As important as that alignment is, however, the real differentiator in this new events ecosystem is the ability to actually measure the impact of events in accomplishing those outcomes.

"If you can demonstrate that you understand how to interpret the data, that you can demonstrate how it's made an impact on deal volume and velocity or retention—not only protecting customer churn but retention within your own company—when you understand the currency of the event and can prove the value of it, then yeah, you'll be brought in more into those conversations," Dana Pake explains. "It all depends on whether you can demonstrate value."

For corporate event marketers, measuring value will ultimately lead to bigger budgets and more strategic utilization of events as a marketing strategy, bringing events from a more standalone department to an integral part of the organization's marketing strategy. That bigger seat at the table, in our opinion, will eventually lead to more senior roles specific to event strategy. In the future we expect to see more vice president and senior vice president roles specific to event strategy, and eventually more chief experience officers or chief event officers in the not-too-distant future.

CHAPTER

15

New Skills for a New Title

To be successful in today's rapidly evolving events industry, experience managers will need to master many of the traditional skills associated with event professionals and gain at least some degree of familiarity with others that are not.

Despite the advancements in technology and the switch to virtual and hybrid events, event experience managers are still expected to be able to put together a world-class in-person event, and that expectation won't evaporate anytime soon, even with added responsibilities.

In addition to the capabilities traditionally associated with the role, event experience managers will also need some familiarity with data and technology, sales and marketing, public relations, and human resources. While they don't necessarily need to be experts in these fields, they will need to be able to work with a variety of internal and external stakeholders to produce events that align with desired outcomes, using all the technology tools available. Doing so will require enough fluency with each subject matter to speak the same language and stay on the same page.

Data and Technology

Technology was already emerging as a strategic differentiator for event experience managers prior to the pandemic, but the transition to remote and hybrid events only furthered their value. Producing a virtual or hybrid event is only possible through events technology platforms, and a baseline understanding of what technologies are available and what they are capable of is a necessity in this new environment.

As Dana Pake explains, event experience managers don't need to know how the technology works so much as they need to demonstrate some understanding of how technology can be used to solve specific problems. She believes that is because the technology landscape in the events industry is still very much fragmented, and organizers often need to utilize a broad range of tools in order to achieve desired outcomes. "It's still a Frankensteined approach to custom-build the solution you need to achieve how you want your event to perform," she says. "A strategist really has to understand the tech stack, what to bring in when to solve which problem."

Event experience manager and consultant Monique Ruff-Bell, who has worked on major global events including Money 20/20 and Cannes-Lions, echoed that sentiment. She believes every event experience manager needs some fluency in the language of data and technology in order to succeed. "Does everyone have to be an event technologist? Absolutely not," she says. "Do they need to have an understanding of some core aspects so they can help pitch in, help take over, be flexible about participating in helping to deliver this stuff? Yes."

Monique believes every event experience manager and event team member should aim for a technology literacy rate of about 20 percent, as compared to the knowledge of a designated event technologist. That includes both a baseline understanding of technology tools that can help achieve business outcomes, as well as a baseline understanding of data and how it can be used to measure and optimize event performance.

"It's all about how you can use data to further the business," she says. "If you are just saying I have this wonderful way of capturing all of this data, but you're not using it outside of the event business, or you're not using it for other parts of the business, great, you've got the data, but someone has to figure out the value of that data."

Colleen Bisconti of IBM puts it even more bluntly: "We're no longer event marketers; we're digital event marketers, like it or not. None of us signed up for this, but that's what we are." She explains, "We cannot be strong, effective, impactful event marketers unless we use data, understand data, analyze the data, and let that drive our decisions, fundamentally. I don't care what industry you're in or how big your company is, that is table stakes."

Understanding how to read a dashboard, knowing how to sift through data to find answers to specific problems, and knowing what data to collect in the first place are all highly valuable skills every event experience manager will need in order to succeed.

Applying Tech Industry Design Principles

As an event experience manager for a company focused on software development, Dana Pake sees this new technology-focused aspect of the job through the lens of product design and user experience, two key principles of successfully bringing a software product to market.

"We talk a lot in events about what the attendee journey map looks like, but applying the lens of UX [user experience] discipline on that would make folks stand out," she says. "Events are products, and during my time heading up events at InVision, I learned that every event is a prototype, and we're going to come in with an assumption around a problem, and we're going to design around that, and then we're going to produce the event. And we'll get some of it right, and a lot of it wrong, and then we'll optimize and do it again."

The concept of producing a minimum viable product and then iterating and improving on that product is quite common in the development of technology products, and Dana recommends applying similar principles to event design. Whether you work in the tech industry or not, understanding how to design a minimum viable product, how to effectively test it, and how to continually iterate and improve on the initial design are all key traits of effective event experience managers today.

Sales and Marketing

As event experience managers focus their efforts on aligning events with business outcomes—for their own companies or their sponsors and exhibitors—the majority of those outcomes will be tied to sales and marketing efforts. In order to succeed as an event experience manager, you therefore need a certain level of fluency in those fields.

As Monique Ruff-Bell puts it, event professionals have always benefited from having some understanding of *how* their activities further broaden sales and marketing efforts. Now, she argues, they must become "commercially minded" and be able to apply a sales and marketing lens to every aspect of their event.

"There's a lot of people that do not come to the table understanding how revenue is generated from events, or they don't understand how to service your delegates and your sponsors to make sure they're willing to invest in your event products," she says. "It's extremely important."

Moving forward, event experience managers will be required to have some base level understanding of how their events fit into broader sales and marketing strategies *and* how to utilize sales and marketing strategies to achieve better outcomes for events themselves. That means having a baseline understanding of go-to market strategists and product launches, the event's email marketing, landing pages, video content, and more. It also requires a strong understanding of the sales and marketing funnel, account-based marketing (ABM), and how events tie directly into sales and marketing objectives.

Furthermore, event experience managers should be prepared to utilize data that speaks to sales and marketing efforts. Sales and marketing teams, sponsors, and exhibitors respond to metrics like lead generation, brand awareness, or market penetration. Understanding these common key performance indicators (KPIs) will help bridge the gap between event strategy and broader sales and marketing efforts of stakeholders.

Human Resources

While events are often designed around achieving specific sales and marketing outcomes for the enterprise, they are also often closely tied to human resources as well. That is because events are considered a key tool for attracting talent, employee retention, culture, and camaraderie.

As with technology, sales, and marketing teams, event experience managers should also be able to speak the language of human resources and be prepared to work with HR teams to achieve their stated outcomes. Understanding the way in which events contribute to the employee experience, or how they further the company culture, should be a key consideration in event strategy.

Take, for instance, Amazon Career Day, Amazon's annual event for attracting new employees and educating current ones. In 2021, the event provided nearly 30,000 personalized career-coaching sessions with participants and thought leadership presentations. As part of Career Day, over one million people applied for a job at Amazon.[1]

---

[1] https://www.yahoo.com/now/amazon-career-day-2021.

Public Relations

Events send a signal to the outside world about what a brand stands for. Moving forward, we envision event experience managers working closely with brand, sponsor, and exhibitor public relations teams as an extension of their sales and marketing efforts. While PR teams are less concerned with bottom-line sales figures, they are tasked with maintaining a positive brand image. Understanding the basics of PR strategy and how events can further those goals is a great attribute for event experience managers to bring to the table.

Apple's product events have long served as a textbook example of how events can be leveraged to drive PR goals. At these events, conducted several times throughout a year, Apple executives announce the latest hardware and software offerings, resulting in a flurry of speculation leading up to each event and extensive media coverage following afterward.

Digital Content Production

The transition from in-person to virtual and hybrid events requires event experience managers to develop new skills and capabilities related to producing quality digital content. While most event experience managers have a working knowledge of producing content for the live stage, they've recently had to work in an entirely new arena, and the virtual format isn't likely going away soon. As many also discovered during the pandemic, virtual content is distinct from in-person content, and digital audiences behave differently than those attending in person.

As a result, it is incumbent on event experience managers to have a high degree of comfort producing content in a virtual format. Managers must acquire a strong understanding of video products, of video streaming platforms and technologies, of virtual audience interaction and engagement, and of how to maintain virtual audience engagement.

"People need to understand how individuals are consuming content digitally, and how you apply that to your audience or to your journey," says Colleen Bisconti of IBM, adding that producing virtual content requires more than simply reducing the length of events and sessions. "It's easy for people to say our conference was four days so we'll make it three days; people are really challenged to apply digital behavior to what the future of events should look like."

To complicate things further, these principles are often a moving target, as innovations in social media often trickle down into other forms of digital content. For example, a 2016 study found that 85 percent of videos are viewed without sound, inspiring a transition toward subtitles (Patel, 2016). As another example, a study from 2018 found that 70 percent of millennials won't turn their phone horizontally to watch a video (Bennett, 2018), inspiring a transition from horizontal to vertical videos (Peters, 2019). More recently, the popularity of temporary "story" format videos has created a preference for shorter form and even lower-budget productions, while TikTok's meteoric rise has inspired more quick cuts, "challenge" style videos, and even more influencer-driven content (Savage, 2018).

Social media platforms are constantly evolving, and they often set the tone for viewer expectations when it comes to virtual content. Staying on top of these trends, understanding the basics of broadcast production, and integrating virtual and in-person audiences will all be key attributes of the event experience manager of the future.

16

Soft Skills

Having the technical know-how to get the job done is only one part of the equation and, depending on whom you ask, a small part at that. In the past century or so, there has been a gradually building recognition that what makes people successful in their careers, and in life, has little to do with their academic field, grade point average, or even their IQ.

In contrast to acquiring the "hard skills" that require specific technical abilities, managers need to possess competencies in the areas of communication, collaboration, emotional intelligence, grit, creativity, adaptability, and emotional intelligence. These attributes are most commonly referred to as *soft skills* but are also sometimes referred to as *human skills*, *people skills*, or *social and emotional skills*. Whatever you call them, these skills encompass a wide variety of capabilities that are typically more representative of character and personality than academic prowess. In just about any field, but especially in the events industry, being successful requires a strong balance of both hard and soft skills.

A Brief History of Soft Skills

In 1918, author Charles Riborg Mann published a report for the Carnegie Foundation titled *A Study of Engineering Education*, which was intended to determine what made an engineering student successful in a future career and encompassed a range of necessary skills and proficiencies. Mann ultimately concluded that only 15 percent of a person's career success was the result of technical knowledge; the remaining 85 percent was the result of interpersonal skills.

The term *soft skills* was later developed by the U.S. military between 1968 and 1972 to represent those nontechnical skills Mann was referring to, as the military sought to better define what made an individual soldier or unit more successful than others (Wright, 2018). After determining that attributes like leadership, communication, and teamwork were equally or more valuable than the ability to operate equipment and machinery, the military formally defined *soft skills* as "important job-related skills which involve little or no interaction with machines."

In 1990, two psychology professors—John D. Mayer of the University of New Hampshire and Peter Salovey of Yale University—coined a new term to represent a specific subset of soft skills that encompassed traits like empathy, collaboration, and emotional maturity. They eventually settled on the term *emotional intelligence*, defining it as "the ability to accurately perceive your own and others' emotions; to understand the signals that emotions send about relationships; and to manage your own and others' emotions."

In the ensuing decades, many scholars and management organizations studied these skills and advanced our understanding of their value—most notably Daniel Goleman in his best-selling book *Emotional Intelligence* (1995), and its follow-up, *Working with Emotional Intelligence* (2000). As research into the field of nonacademic skills became more popular, the business community gradually began incorporating those learnings into their methodologies. Thanks to these highly popular studies and books, the movement really started to pick up steam in the 1990s, and by the dawn of the tech boom in the early 2000s, *soft skills* had become a common buzzword in the tech industry vernacular.

By 2014, the emphasis on soft skills was no longer a fringe idea in the business world beyond Silicon Valley. According to a survey conducted that year under the guidance of CareerBuilder, 77 percent of employers indicated that soft skills like work ethic, dependability, attitude, and self-motivation were just as important as hard skills. In 2018, researchers had concluded that emotional intelligence was twice as important as technical and cognitive ability in distinguishing top performers from average ones, and for senior leaders it was four times as important.

Whatever doubt remained regarding the value of soft skills largely evaporated in 2020 and 2021, when workers and managers had to overcome an array of challenges related to the pandemic.

How the Pandemic Cemented the Value of Soft Skills

As the pandemic forced businesses to rapidly change their practices and adapt to an uncertain situation, soft skills took center stage. Many organizations had championed the value of soft skills in their recruiting and training practices in the preceding years, but for most, the pandemic was the first major test of those efforts. Making it through that tumultuous period required employees and managers to demonstrate a variety of soft skills, such as grit, resiliency, emotional intelligence, empathy, and strong communication.

Those organizations that had hired a truly resilient and empathetic workforce likely fared better than those that were only paying lip service to the value of soft skills, evidenced by how training priorities evolved during that time. According to a 2021 study, conducted by McKinsey, 69 percent of organizations put more emphasis on skill building than they did prior to the pandemic, with more than half focusing on developing leadership, critical thinking, decision-making, and project-management skills (Bouwer, Saxon, and Wittkamp, 2021).

"Compared with the results from 2019, many of the skills where respondents report the biggest increases in focus fall into two categories: social and emotional skills (which account for three of the five biggest increases) and advanced cognitive skills," note the study's authors. "For example, the share saying that their companies are addressing interpersonal skills and empathy skills has nearly doubled in the past year."

Soft skills have been historically difficult to develop and measure, as compared with more traditional hard skills. In the past, many assumed that such "life skills" developed naturally through lived experiences. That is in large part due to the way in which academic programs are structured. Most institutions have a long history of teaching and testing subjects like math and science and assumed softer skills were developed independently, outside of the classroom.

More recently, however, there is a growing recognition that not only can soft skills be taught and developed, but they can also be put to the test in job interviews. Fortunately, curriculums have gradually begun to catch up, with new training and development programs structured around soft skills becoming more widely available. For those in the events industry, however, there are a few that should be at or near the top of the priority list.

Key Soft Skills for Event Experience Managers

The events industry is not immune to the soft skills revolution taking place in the broader talent marketplace. According to the PCMA study, one-third of event planners cite soft skills as a top area event strategists need to develop in order to be successful during the pandemic recovery period (Russell, 2020). In their study, PCMA specifically notes "resilience in times of crisis" as a timely and relevant skill for event organizers, and the rationale is fairly obvious, given the high levels of uncertainty experienced during that period.

According to event director Monique Ruff-Bell, the pandemic may be nearing its end, but the possibility of another major disruption will forever be top of mind. "Let's say we went through another pandemic, god forbid, [event experience managers are] going to have to be comfortable in being flexible and pivoting," she says.

What follows is a discussion of a few of the most important soft skills event experience managers should focus on in order to be successful in the future.

Empathy

The pandemic put a spotlight on a number of soft skills, but when considering the experiences of the past two years, many would cite empathy as the most valuable trait in difficult and uncertain times.

According to Dana Pake, in the early days of the pandemic, the scramble to move events to an online format was often approached as a technical challenge—an arms race to develop quality digital content. She fears that in the midst of the chaos many forgot the real purpose of events and why people attend. "What I've found with what happened with virtual was that there was this over index on content without understanding that the event is really about connecting people," she says. "When I think about it from that lens, it's about empathy for the attendee, what they're trying to achieve."

Empathy is often cited as an important characteristic for positions within industries of all shapes and sizes, but as a role dedicated to inspiring and engaging people, event experience managers must develop a strong degree of empathy to be successful.

The Ability to Solve Problems Creatively

Producing a live event requires a high degree of creative problem solving, and while the industry has long valued those who can think on their feet, the pandemic has further emphasized this value.

"At the end of the day, the best event people are problem solvers," says Dana Pake. "We solve problems at a high strategic level—like what is the problem we're trying to solve for the company in terms of objectives; what are the problems we're trying to solve for the attendee; why they will come and invest their time, money, and energy with us; we are also solving problems on the fly, because it's not if it will go wrong, but what will go wrong—so this ability to be agile, to make it work, to solve the problem, that's our job."

Moving forward, Dana believes that the ability to solve problems using creative solutions will become even more valuable for event experience managers. She explains that deeper integration with broader sales and marketing efforts will require event experience managers to develop creative solutions for achieving overall business goals.

The transition to virtual events and a more competitive event landscape will also require event experience managers to become more creative in solving problems for attendees in order to develop and maintain engagement. Furthermore, increased experimentation with—and reliance on—virtual platforms will require strategists to solve even more complex problems on the fly, in both physical and virtual environments.

The Ability to Manage Uncertainty

In the age of disruption, and in the wake of a major global disruption, event experience managers will have to demonstrate a certain degree of comfort with uncertainty. Unfortunately, this goes against our natural tendency to prefer order and predictability, but the reality is that our world is chaotic and unpredictable, especially now. Dana Pake believes event experience managers will need to demonstrate an ability to remain calm under pressure and to effectively navigate through disruption. "You've got to get comfortable with being uncomfortable," she says. "You're going to get shit wrong, and that's okay; it's the process of just trying and learning."

Dana explains that the industry is undergoing a period of rapid change and innovation, and in order to succeed in this new environment, event experience managers need to be comfortable experimenting and tinkering and treating the inevitable failures as a learning opportunity. "Innovation means there's going to be failure, and you're going to have to be calculated with your risks so you're failing in the right ways," she says. "You'll have to get comfortable with being uncomfortable, and learn to adapt."

The concept of adaptability, according to Dana, goes hand in hand with managing uncertainty. She explains that GitHub, for example, operates under the principle of "Ship to Learn," which she says is developer-speak for emphasizing progress over perfection.

"You've got to move with speed and you've got to have that appetite to just adapt," she says. "You have to adapt to a global pandemic, you've got to adapt to changing business needs, you've got to understand 'what does my minimum viable program need to look like and how do I save the space to adapt the things I can't even predict right now?'"

Learning not only how to work with uncertainty, but how to operate in a way that allows you to react and adapt effectively to sudden disruption, is a vital trait for event experience managers today.

Communication Skills

Events have long been an elaborate exercise in communication, from communicating a brand's message to communicating a speaker's ideas to communicating the value of a product or service.

Beyond this huge emphasis on external communications, however, event professionals have long been tasked with communicating their ideas, communicating their needs, and communicating effectively among their fellow team members.

The pandemic, however, has only furthered the necessity of strong communication and the array of platforms through which we communicate. During that period just about everyone, including event experience managers, had to learn to communicate effectively over digital platforms, such as video and instant messaging.

Communication skills are so vital to success in just about every role and job type that they remain the most sought-after skill on job applications today, and by a significant margin. Strong communication skills were once considered just an important attribute of sales, customer service, and other customer-facing professionals, but now there is a broader recognition of their importance in just about every role.

As event organizers evolve to become event experience managers, the value of communication only heightens. No longer are event professionals communicating largely within their own teams; now they need the skills to communicate across departments. Understanding some of the basics of how these teams operate and the language that they use will go a long way in bridging that communication gap. Event experience managers similarly need to be well practiced at communicating their ideas to stakeholders and decision makers, with an emphasis on tying the experiences they create for attendees to achieving real-world business outcomes.

"Event leaders have to be really good presenters and storytellers; they have to really convey the value and be able to articulate the strategy and vision of the event to collect cross-alignment across the business," explains Bizzabo's vice president of global events, Devin Cleary.

Devin explains that getting buy-in is a vital part of the event success equation, adding that strategists are often required to do what he refers to as "an internal road show" to present their ideas to various stakeholders and departments. "That's usually the most friction and time-consuming thing we experience in the industry, making sure everyone agrees to move forward with X budget, X plan, X strategy, and making sure that everyone's input is collected, processed, and translated with how we go to market," he says.

Active Listening

Active listening is a similarly vital skill for event experience managers, which goes hand in hand with strong communication skills. Beyond presenting their own ideas, strategists need to be equally as skilled at collecting feedback and incorporating the needs and concerns of others into their processes.

According to Devin Cleary, "Listening to feedback is really critical, especially with the cross alignment; it's really important that you get to the nature of what people are asking for or what they're hoping to accomplish. A lot of the time they might not be as direct as you need them to be, so having active listening skills is really half the battle."

In this new environment, strong communication and active listening skills can be used to develop account-based marketing (ABM) strategies alongside sales and marketing teams, get executive or board buy-in, and develop clear instructions and lines of communication—all key attributes of a successful event experience manager.

Collaboration Skills

Being able to communicate effectively with various stakeholders and departments is only the first step; event experience managers need to demonstrate a strong ability to collaborate with them as well. While communication refers to the ability to speak the same language when exchanging thoughts and ideas, collaboration refers to the ability to execute those thoughts and ideas in tandem with others, even without direct consultation.

As event teams evolve from their previously siloed position to become more integrated with other departments, strategists will need to develop an ability to integrate the needs and concerns of others. For example, Monique Ruff-Bell explains that in this more collaborative environment, each decision has the potential to impact other teams and departments, requiring events professionals to consider others' needs alongside their own. "That is very important for any well-run program to happen; everyone has to be on the same page, and everyone has to understand how everyone is affected by everyone else's delivery on things," she says.

Monique adds that she has personally sought to break up silos within her event teams in order to deliver a successful event and emphasizes that strong collaboration shouldn't be a foreign concept to any effective event experience manager.

"My content team has to work with my sales team; my sales team has to work with my marketing team, because that helps to drive leads for us to bring in sponsorship; my ops team has to work with the sales team on deliverables and has to work with the content team with what we need onsite," she says. "Collaboration should have always been the foundation for your events department, and it needs to continue, and if you weren't doing it before, you should have been."

In a more digital environment, however, Monique believes that there is an even greater need to understand and account for the needs of others. "With the digital aspect that's coming into it, now more than ever, there are so many different things to stay on top of to make sure the digital thing happens and you're still on top of the physical, that it would be scandalous not to have that collaboration happening, and having someone drop the ball and affecting everything," she says.

CHAPTER

17

The New Path for Event Professionals

As event teams are increasingly tasked with collaborating more directly with other departments, we believe the industry as a whole will come to recognize the value of having a broader diversity of skills and experiences within their ranks.

The higher premium placed on a diversity of skills—as opposed to the traditional value attributed to a high degree of proficiency in a single area—is a trend that has impacted a range of industries and roles in recent years. It's why many employers are more open to nontraditional backgrounds when recruiting talent and why the most direct path from education to career isn't always straightforward.

Historically, if you wanted to be a marketer, or a salesperson, or a human resources professional, the best pathway into those careers was the most direct—namely, a degree and prior work experience in that specific field. In recent years, however, more employers have come to prioritize candidates that bring different, more diversified skills to the table.

Now the most employable salesperson, for example, might have earned an undergraduate degree in psychology, spent a few years in human resources, and taken some online courses in sales and marketing. Rather than the candidate with both a bachelor's and master's degree in journalism, the most employable reporter today might have earned a degree in criminology while volunteering for the school paper and spent some years working for a nonprofit before joining the newsroom. Similarly, the most employable human resources professional might have been a high school dropout who ran an independent business for a few years before going back to school.

At Bizzabo we've made a point of ruling out higher-education degrees as requirements in our hiring process, instead prioritizing experience and potential. Our customer-obsessed team boasts former scientists and photographers, holistic medicine professionals and actors, sommeliers, martial artists, and poets.

Through the eyes of a forward-thinking employer, these candidates bring skills and capabilities to the table that likely don't exist within their ranks currently. Rather than being seen as indecisive or unfocused, as they may have been in the past, candidates with an array of experiences are seen as providing an opportunity to enrich their teams with new capabilities and experiences. Rather than everyone working from the same playbook, leaders often prefer to have team members that can lean on their unique backgrounds to draw different conclusions and find more creative solutions.

Furthermore, the growing emphasis on cross-departmental collaboration has put a higher premium on staff with prior experience on related teams. When work was heavily siloed, there was very little value in having team members that had experience working in different departments, but that is no longer the case. In an increasingly collaborative work environment, that diversity of experiences can be vital in breaking down those walls.

Having a broad range of skills and experiences also provides a certain degree of job security. Those who have a high level of expertise in a single area are essentially putting all their eggs in one basket, and in the age of disruption, there really are no safe baskets anymore. Having the ability to pivot careers is the best job security one can have in this new reality.

Monique Ruff-Bell is no stranger to this principle. Though she's been in the events industry for most of her 20-year career, Monique started out as a promotion manager for a bridal magazine, then transitioned into event production, then strategy, then programming, then operations, then planning, then marketing and PR, and eventually content. More recently, she's served as an event director for some of the largest events in the world.

"I remember going to this recruiter having had all these various roles, and she told me you have too much experience in different things within events; I need you to have one road you want to go down, because that's what they're looking for," she says. Monique, however, didn't think her diverse experiences were a disadvantage. "I understand what all the departments need, and what it takes to put on a successful program. It's valuable to have those different experiences, because I have to collaborate with various departments."

Though she was discouraged by the recruiter's comments, Monique continued her job hunt, searching for an employer that would value her less specialized background. "Two months after, someone did get it, and they liked that I had experience in various departments," she says.

Monique adds that this employer is more representative of a new way of thinking about talent in the events industry and beyond. She believes that in a more integrated future, event professionals will be more valued for the unique insights they can offer based on seemingly unrelated prior work experiences.

"You shouldn't be penalized because you switched from sales to ops to content. You have such value because you understand how to work with these various departments," she says. "It is a plus and not a negative, because you will have a better understanding, especially if you're trying to move up into leadership roles, of what it takes to make a full program work."

As an event director and senior brand leader, Monique says she doesn't view the time she spent in positions that ultimately didn't last as a waste of time. Instead, she views them as key building blocks to her current leadership role, believing that event industry leaders should have intimate knowledge of, and direct experience with, a range of roles within and beyond the event team.

Furthermore, Monique says many feel pressured to stick with their roles, even if they don't enjoy them, rather than starting fresh in a new area, often out of fear of falling behind in their careers. What she's discovered through her own experience, however, is that switching roles is only a minor and temporary step backwards, but ultimately makes candidates stronger over the long run.

The Value of a Broader Skill Set

Monique Ruff-Bell says that the pandemic further solidified her opinion on the value of a diverse skill set. She explains that in 2020 the industry was forced to evolve rapidly, creating a wide variety of new roles and opportunities, but rendering others obsolete. For example, Monique says that many event professionals who held positions tied closely to physical events, such as director of sales for hotels, found themselves out of a job during the pandemic. Those who didn't have other skills to offer the event's team, specifically related to virtual and hybrid events, were suddenly at a higher risk of ultimately getting left behind.

"This pandemic was a big moment for our industry; it really showcased how vulnerable we are to our businesses," she says. "I absolutely think it's important that you make sure that you have skills that can match other [needs] within the industry, that you can pivot into something else if need be, to make sure you can put food on the table."

Moving forward, however, Monique strongly believes that experience in both digital and physical event production will be vital in the transition toward more hybrid events. That is why she strongly encourages event experience managers, and especially those interested in pursuing leadership positions in the future, to seek out education and experience in both domains.

"I had ops people who 100 percent hated going virtual. They did not want to learn anything about any type of broadcasting production or anything like that; they loved the feeling of a live event. Some of them I know in the community left and decided to do something else," she says. "If you are going to be in this industry, you have to be open to having combined skills, in the virtual and physical aspects, even from operations."

As the industry continues to incorporate more technology, becomes more integrated with other teams and departments, and moves toward a more hybrid model, the value of those diverse skills and experiences will only increase.

Where Experience Counts

While the industry is evolving toward valuing a broader array of skills and experiences, however, there are limitations to what kind of experience will be considered relevant. According to Bizzabo's vice president of global events, Devin Cleary, event teams still require that their staff are ready to hit the ground running, because tight timelines and budgets make it difficult to get inexperienced staffers up to speed.

"We can overlook if they do not have extensive event experience only if they have things that can translate into the event world," he says. "For example, if they worked in an art gallery, or they participated in a virtual gaming event; if they have life experience that demonstrates they understand how to deliver an experience to a group of people, and that they can deliver on their expectations, that's something we can translate to our field."

Cleary adds that while many of his team members have formal education in the events space, he has personally hired others based on a combination of soft skills and relevant work experience.

"It really comes down to whether you've operated at the level that we're at," he says. "We have a lot of events and never enough talent to support and deliver, so we don't really have time to handhold; everyone really needs to own their discipline and be able to deliver on the work we expect them to deliver on."

The industry has begun finding value in nontraditional backgrounds and experiences that align well with the needs of the event team, but at the end of the day not every educational and career pathway will naturally lead to the events industry. Understanding how to deliver an experience to a live audience and some of the basics of event strategy is still a baseline expectation.

18

The Event Team of the Future

The transition to virtual and hybrid events will ultimately serve to increase the reach, impact, and measurability of events, but achieving those bigger outcomes will require a bigger team. With the addition of a few key roles and expertise, event teams will be better prepared to meet the challenges and seize the opportunities that will result from a more complex and more competitive event landscape.

Beyond the traditional skills and roles that have historically been required to put on a successful in-person event, event teams will now depend on the expertise and resources of professionals dedicated to producing virtual experiences, as well as others who are able to bridge the two. The heightened dependency on data and technology will also necessitate the addition of technologists who can ensure smooth delivery of virtual experiences.

Dana Pake, for one, believes that production teams can potentially be split but need to be unified by an executive producer overseeing continuity. "I'm a minority voice in thinking virtual and in-person events should be decoupled, but you're still producing two events at once, and so you need two teams, and companies need to understand that and give the budgets to these teams," she says. "They're two very distinct experiences, and when people are thinking about hybrid they're constantly thinking about how to tie the two together, and maybe that can happen. People are still experimenting, but I think you need to be prepared to have the digital production team and the IRL production team."

However your team will be structured, there are several roles we believe will be key for creating successful event experiences moving forward. The following sections discuss these roles in relation to the event formats to which they are primarily (but not exclusively) relevant.

The Virtual Events Team

The newest aspect of event production—namely, virtual content—will likely require teams to add many new positions. Given the parallels with traditional live broadcasts, many of the roles that will be required to fulfill this aspect of the event will include skills and experiences similar to those prized by film and television production teams. Meanwhile, other roles will be a result of the increasingly strategic and data-driven nature of event programs. Below are a few of the most important roles that will make up a virtual events team.

Event Technologist

An event technologist is vital to ensuring your team employs the right technology for your event and gets the most out of your technology stack—that is, the compilation of tools and software used by your organization. Event technologists are tasked with staying on top of tech trends and seeking out solutions that can enhance the attendee experience.

As Rexson Serrao shared with us on an episode of the IN-PERSON podcast, the event technologist is key for companies who prize "technology as a differentiator" and who are "focused on innovation."

Event technologists help event organizers surface answers to questions around event integrations and data that event organizers would otherwise be unaware of—often in collaboration with other technical resources within an organization. As Dana Pake puts it, "It's clutch to have an event technologist on your team who can have those deep-in-the-bowels kind of tech conversations, and help the event production team surface what they didn't even know they needed to know."

Event technologists can also help teams solve some of the common issues that virtual events often run into. Dana explains that, just as in-person event teams typically have contingency plans in place in case they run into problems, virtual event teams need someone they can rely on to fix issues as they arise during the actual production and to devise mitigation strategies for potential technical issues. "Before your plan B was the 'rain plan,' what happens if it rains?" she says. "Most event planners are now thinking about what happens when [the event platform] goes down; sometimes they just leave it to their vendor, but you need to go a step further."

Having a dedicated event technologist can therefore not only ensure the smooth delivery of virtual experiences but also take some of the burden for managing the technical aspects away from other team members.

Executive Producer

Taking a few pages out of the broadcaster's playbook, hybrid and virtual events will similarly need someone on the team who has deep knowledge and experience with orchestrating live productions: the executive producer (EP). The job of the event executive producer is to create and deliver content in an engaging manner. To do this, the EP works with a variety of team members to address issues around length, format, style, audio and visual elements, and technology.

Since the beginning of the pandemic, the number of job postings for executive producers within the events industry has exploded, demonstrating both the value they can bring and the competition in the talent marketplace. As Devin puts it, executive producers "were probably the number one job description of 2020 for the events industry."

The role is in such high demand because producing an engaging virtual experience requires a certain degree of professional video production experience. Take, for instance, Spotify's 2021 flagship virtual experience Stream On. The event featured keynotes from executives at Spotify, interviews with Spotify creators (artists featured on the platform), and even performances from celebrities like Justin Bieber. Directing all aspects of the event was Keyana Kashi, global director of experiential and content production at Spotify.

As Keyana shared with us on an episode of the IN-PERSON podcast in June 2021, she tapped into her background working for media production companies like CNN, Discovery Communications, Vevo, and NBCUniversal, to inform decisions that she made around set design, visual language, recording location, and even the types of lenses used for cameras—all with the goal of creating a unified experience for viewers.

Camera and Sound Operators

In the immediate aftermath of the pandemic, virtual events typically featured speakers in their own homes talking into their webcams. Prior to the pandemic, most in-person events settled for a camera or two at the back of the room for capturing video. Given the challenges associated with keeping virtual audiences engaged, however, it's important to utilize strong audio and video tools in order to create a more immersive attendee experience for virtual audiences. That's where camera and sound operators come in.

Their jobs, as the titles imply, are to ensure a crisp, smooth, and enjoyable viewing experience for at-home audiences through video and sound production. Rather than a webcam or a couple of cameras at the back of the venue, hybrid events will require multiple camera stations, roving handheld operators, as well as a sound specialist or microphone operator. Having dedicated professionals who can capture high-quality sound and audio will go a long way toward improving the virtual attendee experience, not to mention creating a higher-quality database of content that can be utilized after the event. These roles are often outsourced to agency partners but may also be taken in-house as part of a creative, design, or studio team.

The In-Person Event Team

Most event teams today include event professionals who have spent all or most of their careers producing live events, and while their expertise is still of value, it's important to consider the new capabilities that will be required to orchestrate the in-person aspects of a hybrid event. The key difference is that the event itself no longer exists primarily for in-person audiences.

As events evolve to include virtual attendees, the in-person portion will begin to resemble the live audiences in a broadcast studio. Below are a few of the professionals that you'll need on your team in order to elevate your in-person events from a standalone experience to one that caters to both in-person and virtual audiences.

Moderator

In-person events have long featured a dedicated host or moderator who is tasked with introducing speakers and sessions while also interacting with the audience, but it's important to highlight just how vital this position becomes in a hybrid environment. Moderators are no longer tasked with just moving the conversation along; they are now in charge of capturing the attention of a virtual audience as well. In practice, this may look like posing questions for virtual attendees to respond to in chat or bringing virtual attendees "on stage" (on camera) so that they can pose questions to speakers.

Moderators can also help ensure continuity between presentations and give viewers a reason to continue engaging with the event after the session they specifically logged on to has ended. "Moderators draw out the engagement in audiences and they set the pace of the program," said Dana Pake when we spoke with her at our (Almost) HYBRID event in November 2020. "Things can and will go wrong and they can buy you time, or they can speed things up."

At our Agents of Hybrid event in 2021, we were lucky enough to have the acclaimed TV personality and tech expert Katie Linendoll as our host. Given that Agents of Hybrid featured two audiences (a live in-studio audience and a much larger virtual audience), Katie worked with our events team to find novel ways of engaging both. For instance, when the event first started, Katie provided digital viewers with a tour of the event space, stopping to speak to different on-site attendees and Bizzabo team members along the way. When it came to the Q&A segment of sessions, Katie took questions from in-person audience members and also read off questions submitted by virtual attendees with the help of an iPad that she had on hand. Having a dedicated moderator like Katie on-hand helped us engage our audiences while helping us smoothly transition from session to session.

Onsite Technician

Just as it's important to have an event technologist managing the virtual aspects of your hybrid events, it's equally important to have a technician onsite to manage and troubleshoot technical issues at the venue. As events transition toward a broadcast model, they will continue to incorporate more technologies and tools, and having someone onsite who can manage video streaming and other onsite technologies is vital. An onsite technician can also help step in to assist with Wi-Fi, microphones, slide decks, and other technical aspects of the onsite experience.

The Hybrid Events Team

While you may find it helpful to create dedicated event teams for in-person and virtual events, it is important to incorporate dedicated staff who can help bridge the two. Those who sit between the two sides of the event team are also well positioned to collaborate with other internal stakeholders and help ensure events are meeting expectations and solving real business needs. Below are a few of the most important hybrid positions event teams will need to incorporate in order to be successful in a hybrid environment.

Audience Development/Event Marketer

Event teams have long utilized marketing expertise on their staff to publicize their events and drive registrations, but in a hybrid environment, and with the introduction of more virtual marketing tools, their role will expand to incorporate both virtual and live experiences. According to Devin Cleary, event teams typically relied on their internal marketing ecosystems to drive registration, but moving forward he believes more teams will need a dedicated marketer on their staff as events increasingly become dedicated brands or products unto themselves.

We are already seeing this transformation underway with established event brands like Forbes, Bloomberg, HubSpot, and Salesforce designating marketing directors, audience development managers, and event marketing managers to focus solely on marketing and promotion for events.

As events become more purposeful and more measurable, event teams will increasingly benefit from dedicated digital marketing professionals in their ranks, rather than relying on the expertise of marketers elsewhere in their organization.

Event Experience Manager

The event experience manager is both a universal title that speaks to the changing responsibilities of event planners and also a unique role that we predict event leaders will hire for their teams. For an analogue, look to customer support. For many years, B2B customer support was a function designed to solve problems that customers were facing. However, changes in consumer expectations and needs called for an evolution in how B2B organizations managed their relationships with their customers. The result was the advent of the *customer success manager*, a dedicated staff member charged with proactively serving customers in addition to the more reactive support provided by dedicated support teams.

Similarly, in the events space, the event experience manager is the answer to the experience-focused nature of the attendees and other stakeholders today. The event experience manager is the staff member dedicated to managing, auditing, and taking responsibility for delivering a great stakeholder experience. This role is especially critical in a hybrid context, where event teams are tasked with providing distinct but cohesive customer experiences in both a virtual and in-person context.

"You need an overall auditor on your team who is really doing the due diligence in conjunction with the VP or above, who is spinning a lot of plates in the air; they need someone 100 percent focused, 24/7, on what is the experience of the entire program," says Devin. "Every member of the team needs to look at it through that lens, but like a project manager, you need accountability, you need someone who is only focused on that, so we don't drop the ball on one aspect of the program."

Technology

CHAPTER

19

The Changing Event Technology Landscape

The pandemic was a transformational period not only for those in the trenches adopting new skills to orchestrate unique virtual experiences. During that time, those of us who work on the technology side of things were also going through a transformative period of our own.

In only a matter of months, we watched as a once small group of event technology vendors ballooned to encompass a range of new players, including some that probably didn't consider themselves in the event technology space previously. Just as the pandemic opened the door to new opportunities for event teams that were able to adapt quickly, it similarly required technology providers like Bizzabo to evolve at breakneck speed to meet the needs of the industry. It wasn't just the underlying technology that had to change, but the way we see ourselves as a company and an industry.

Whether virtual or hybrid, the event platform is really the central infrastructure where everything happens. It is not just where the data flows or the content is housed; it is now the headquarters of the actual experience itself.

During 2020 and 2021, we found ourselves among many companies—some familiar to this space, others not—racing to develop new capabilities that would meet the needs of event teams in the virtual and hybrid era. Now that technology has become so intertwined with event success, it is incumbent on event experience managers to understand how event technology has evolved in recent years. Event managers must acquire an understanding of certain tools and capabilities, the important distinctions between platforms, and how to approach the task of finding the right technology partner in the virtual and hybrid era.

Expansion and Consolidation

Prior to the pandemic, most event technology providers fell into one of two buckets: point or all-in-one solutions. Point solutions offered a specific tool to help solve a specific need, such as email marketing, agenda building, website modules, content management systems, registration, data management, and more. All-in-one solutions, as the name implies, sought to provide all (or most) of these solutions within a single platform.

Back then, there were just a handful of major point solutions to choose from and an even smaller number of all-in-one solutions like ours, with roughly 10 to 15 total players in the entire market. To be sure, there was still significant investment in event technology happening during this time. In 2016, a privately held investment firm called Vista Equity Partners purchased Cvent, an event management software provider founded in the 1990s, for $1.65 billion. The same investment fund purchased another legacy solution, Lanyon, for $1.05 billion. Following the purchase of both solutions, Vista Equity merged Lanyon into Cvent. The new company retains Cvent's name, headquarters, and CEO.

Eventually, many smaller technology firms were not able to survive. In some cases, their only path was either to sell or to merge with another organization that had more funding. Cvent, for instance, acquired Social Tables, Kapow, and QuickMobile. The legacy platform Aventri (formerly branded as etouches) followed suit, acquiring ITN International, Loopd, Zentila, and TapCrowd.

We saw a similar cycle, although with much higher stakes, emerge during the pandemic, when event experience leaders were suddenly tasked with onboarding streaming, digital registration, virtual network, content libraries, and other solutions. As a result of the increase in demand, the number of players in the event technology space swelled in 2020. It grew to encompass the long-time incumbents and new start-ups, as well as a sizable number of others that would never have considered themselves in the event industry previously.

In those days, event technology was specific to things like registration and agenda-building software, event apps, and websites, but the event itself still existed in a physical space. During the pandemic, the definition of *event technology* expanded and now encompasses a range of providers that were not previously associated with events. For instance, video-conferencing tools like Zoom or Microsoft Teams, webinar hosting platforms, and livestreaming video platforms had not been considered part of the events industry, at least not directly. That all changed in 2020.

Event tech is no longer being looked at strictly within the confines of events. More and more often, event professionals are speaking of event software in the same way they would speak of marketing technology platforms (MarTech) like Salesforce, Marketo, or HubSpot. Likewise, event teams (and the larger organizations in which they exist) are beginning to regard event technology with the same significance that had been traditionally reserved for MarTech.

Feeding into this frenzy of new event solutions has been an eager investor landscape that saw the promise of virtual and hybrid events and an industry that was scrambling to adapt to new business conditions. According to a study we conducted in 2020, 93 percent of event professionals intended to invest in virtual events moving forward, and a report by Allied Market Research predicts the events industry will grow an average of 11.2 percent each year between 2021 and 2028.

While it's difficult to pinpoint the exact dollar value of those investments—as the definition of event technology has expanded to encompass a wider range of providers—this period saw eager investors betting big on event technology companies.

After this period of rapid expansion, however, another contraction occurred, as the later stages of the pandemic began to see considerable consolidation. In May 2021, Cisco announced the closing of their acquisition of Slido, an event engagement tool, and their intent to acquire the event platform Socio. In July 2021, Hopin acquired the event marketing platform Attendify, and the event software provider Bevy acquired the event management software company Eventtus. And in August 2021, the technology-enabled services company Intrado acquired the event management company Hubb.

At Bizzabo, we've participated in this consolidation of the market as well but from a different angle. Unlike other event software companies that have acquired complete event technology solutions, we have sought out premiere products, technologists, and infrastructure to holistically incorporate the most cutting-edge capabilities into our Event Experience OS.

In May 2021, we acquired Whalebone, a Swedish technology start-up that enhances the experience between speakers and their audiences to humanize digital interactions. The technology makes it possible for speakers to hear and visualize virtual crowds. Whalebone's Crowd Amplification gives speakers immediate, real-time feedback from their attendees to help them interpret audience sentiment and excitement. Attendees can show their appreciation and support virtually and can experience the shared excitement of the entire audience. Data collected generates highly responsive sounds and produces an immersive visualization of the crowd, providing a bird's-eye view of the audience and its interactions, cultivating a more intimate, shared experience.

In June 2021, we announced our acquisition of x.ai, a powerful artificial intelligence scheduling tool designed to automate tedious meeting elements. It generates compatible meeting times across time zones, sends follow-ups/reminders, and manages cancellations automatically. The engine empowers event participants to make meaningful connections at virtual, in-person, and hybrid events.

And in October 2021, we announced the acquisition of interactive event production platform TeeVid to help Bizzabo customers create immersive TV-like experiences for every type of event. Notably, the team at TeeVid has built a fully independent video infrastructure, leveraging open-source technologies alongside proprietary code.

As investment increased alongside competition, major players in this space began a wave of acquisitions intended to help increase their digital offerings and further the integration of virtual and live experiences.

Why Event Technology Matters

All of this is to say that staying on top of the latest technological developments, understanding what's possible, and determining how to match the right solution with your needs as an event professional have all become a lot more complicated. While it's an exciting time to be an event professional, with new technologies providing new capabilities, meeting the challenges of this period will require a deeper understanding of a quickly changing technology landscape.

As we outlined in Part 1 of this book, the lack of intuitive and flexible tools that empower organizers to design unique experiences in the hybrid world is one of the four key challenges posed by the Event Impact Gap™.

Prior to the pandemic, event technology existed to help facilitate a live experience. Even if the event technology wasn't great, the event could still prove successful through other redeeming qualities. In a virtual and hybrid environment, however, choosing the right technology vendor becomes at least as important as choosing the right venue for your in-person event.

Moving forward, event experience managers will have to put more time and effort into choosing the right platform to fulfill their needs, execute their strategy, and achieve desired outcomes. Event technology is no longer just a tool that can help them execute a certain task, but a primary enabler of those new opportunities to engage, measure, and manage. In other words, technology vendors are becoming an extension of the internal events team. As a result, choosing a technology vendor should be a little bit like hiring a new employee.

CHAPTER
20

Choosing the Right Technology Partner

In the era of virtual and hybrid events, event professionals have a wealth of opportunities available to maximize their events programming. The only limitation is their imagination—and the capabilities of their technology partners.

But before considering which providers can best help you achieve your goals, it's important to start with a strong definition of what those goals are and how you intend to measure them. Here we would also encourage you to think bigger, and differently, about your events portfolio. The pandemic has served to reinvigorate an industry that has long resisted change, and now is the time to reconsider everything—from how you've always done things to why you do them in the first place.

Questions to Ask When Determining Event Technology Needs

Below are key questions to ask yourself and your team before considering which event technology solution will best suit your needs.

What type of event or events are we hosting? Events are no longer just one thing, or even just three things. While we now tend to think of virtual, in-person, and hybrid as the three options, it's important to recognize that hybrid events exist on a spectrum. Some might be largely in person with a smaller emphasis on virtual attendees, while others might be mostly digital with in-person elements to enhance that virtual experience. Before committing to a technology partner, it's important to consider where your events will land on the spectrum and which vendors are best equipped to facilitate that experience.

How will we measure success?   Before choosing a technology partner, it's important to define the outcomes you want to drive, as well as how you'll ultimately measure your progress toward achieving them. If, for example, success is based around attendee experiences, it's important to look for features and attributes that can help drive, and measure, that experience. If, however, success is measured by sponsorship opportunities, you should favor an event technology platform that is designed to facilitate great sponsorship engagement and experiences.

Who is our audience?   The event technology you use should also be dictated by the audience you want to reach. For example, if you're hosting more niche industry events, you may want to favor a technology platform that is designed to facilitate the type of learning experiences you want to offer your audience. If, however, you want to offer attendees a range of experiences, you should instead favor platforms that are equipped to offer different experience types to different audience members, based on their unique preferences.

What is the expected size and scope of our events?   Virtual and hybrid events are no longer limited by geography, and while some event technology platforms are designed for scale, others could crumble under the weight of too many users. Furthermore, having technical support in multiple time zones and geographies could prove vital in a more global event landscape. Before choosing a technology partner, ask yourself: Will you be hosting

100 attendees or 100,000? Will they all be based in one country, one continent, or all over the world? Understanding the desired size and scope of your events portfolio should play a significant role in determining which technology vendor is equipped to meet your needs.

What kind of experience do we want to facilitate? Given that virtual attendees will interact with your event only through technology platforms, it's important to consider what kind of virtual experience you want to provide. Even for in-person audiences, much of the attendee experience will be dictated by the technology you use. Ask yourself: What is the balance of virtual and in-person attendance? What kind of virtual experience do we intend to facilitate? What kind of in-person experience are we trying to facilitate? How are we going to create a seamless hybrid experience that bridges the gap between the two?

How will we extract ongoing value from our events? Events once existed in a single space and location, but now event teams have the opportunity to extract ongoing value from their events portfolio. When considering your event strategy, it's important to factor in how you'll utilize your library of digital content and which platforms are best equipped to help you leverage them to their fullest.

What solutions currently exist in the market? The market is very fragmented right now, with different vendors offering different types of products and services. As you consider onboarding a new technology partner, consider whether the platform you're evaluating can offer a truly end-to-end solution, one that can handle all of your basic needs as well as the bells and whistles. It's also important to stay on top of industry trends and emerging technologies to stay up to date on what's possible, and practical, with the technology available today.

Are our tech vendors in our corner?   Perhaps the most important question to consider is whether you can trust your vendors to provide the level of customer support you need when things inevitably go wrong. Before working with a new vendor, it's always best to consult reviews and testimonials, or speak with existing customers, with a focus on things like response time, crisis management practices, customer service, and the level of in-house expertise that can help with troubleshooting.

Save More Seats at the Negotiation Table

Prior to the pandemic, the event team often operated within a silo, but in the age of virtual and hybrid events more stakeholders now need a seat at the table when it comes time to select an events success platform. Event teams are now working closely with stakeholders from operations, IT, and marketing departments and—as we have seen—are in some cases hiring dedicated team members to take on these responsibilities. All of these stakeholders are now often involved in the process of evaluating event technology.

Having additional stakeholders also requires a longer timeline for decision-making. Previously, event teams would dedicate a month to a month and a half for evaluating technology vendors, but we've observed that stakeholders now often need more time to make that key decision.

As event success becomes more closely tied to event technology, and as the number of bidders continues to increase as a result of market expansion, teams are now dedicating upwards of two and a half months to choosing their events success platform.

In our experience on the vendor side, we've often seen a three-week review cycle with the internal committee. This committee can include event leaders as well as IT staff and other extended work streams or task forces identified within the business. In some cases, this may include the CIO, CFO, or members of different departments participating in an event program.

In short, an internal committee for vetting event technology can amount to a small army. Once the committee has convened, they will typically narrow down their options to the top three or four contenders and invite each to do a presentation to answer some follow-up questions. Afterwards, the committee will usually invite the top two contenders back for a final interview, where stakeholders will have a chance to go over some of the finer details.

Once a winner is selected, it's time to start the negotiation process, complete a letter of intent and statement of work (SOW), and sign on the dotted line. With a little luck, you'll have a new vendor within a couple of months.

Consider Depth, Breadth, and Experience

In the past, shopping for an event technology platform was relatively simple. Organizers would typically come up with a checklist of key features and capabilities that they needed to achieve their event goals and would consult a small handful of potential vendors to see which checked the most boxes.

In this more complex ecosystem, however, checking the boxes on features and capabilities is only one of many considerations. Event teams should also consider the depth, breadth, and experience that each vendor brings to the table, by which we mean not just looking at what tools they offer, but examining how those features influence the attendee experience at a more granular level.

In this more crowded technology landscape, there are more providers offering all-in-one or end-to-end solutions with the same primary tools and services—such as ticketing and registration, agenda building, and speaker profiles. Despite listing the same tools and features, however, not all of these platforms are created equal. For example, some agenda builders provide users with a long list of sessions they can attend and the option to click to add them to their personalized schedules. Other, more advanced tools, however, will offer search capabilities by subject matter, speaker, time, or keyword, and some will even offer an advanced AI tool that can provide recommendations based on individual attendee preferences.

When it comes to attendee engagement tools, as another example, basic features like a Q&A function and chats are now table stakes. While you might be able to offer a Q&A function, it's important to consider whether attendee questions are posed as text or whether attendees can actually be brought onto the virtual stage to ask their questions via live video stream. Such engagement tools are especially important now as organizers are tasked with bridging the gap between virtual and in-person audiences.

For each of these primary tools and features, it is no longer enough to just check the box. Instead, it is incumbent on event experience managers to consider the depth, breadth, and attendee experience provided by these features. Rather than starting with a list of needs, as was common in the past, event experience managers today need to start with a clear understanding of the experience they want to offer their attendees—and the goals of their organization. Once you establish a clear set of goals and needs, dig a little deeper to consider how the various tools and features will contribute to, or detract from, that experience.

In our experience, this usually comes after the initial request for proposal (RFP) process, where an event organizer will solicit bids from competing event software vendors. When you first send out an RFP, you're likely asking vendors to check the boxes in order to submit a proposal. This is phase 1: just making sure a platform can actually deliver on what you're proposing. Phase 2 is diving deeper into the next level of evaluation and demoing and testing.

In virtual-only events, your platform also serves as the venue itself, so it's important for event experience managers and event teams to conduct that broader examination of the technology landscape to gain a better sense of what's possible. During that process, event teams may elect to bring some of their existing customers into the conversation, either through a focus group or a steering committee, to let them validate the decisions that are being made. Event teams can also survey their attendees to get a better sense of the tools and features they care most about and run some experiments to get a better sense of how those tools and features will be experienced by attendees before settling on a technology partner.

As you navigate through this new and growing event technology landscape, it's important to recognize that features are no longer the be-all and end-all. A platform having a feature means less in today's more advanced ecosystem, because there is a wide range in usability and value offered by the same features on different platforms.

Know Where You Land in the Data Ownership Debate

A thorough examination of the event technology landscape today requires event experience managers to be aware of an ongoing debate taking shape within the events technology landscape more broadly. While this debate has largely taken place behind the scenes, it has the potential to dramatically impact the potential value and usability of your event platform.

The debate is over data, specifically who owns the data that is generated from events. As discussed in Part 2, data has emerged as a key enabler of event success on multiple fronts, from improving internal processes to improving the attendee experience to broader utilizing within the marketing and sales function. Data is a vital resource, and as such there is a contentious debate raging in our community over who gets to own and utilize events data.

In some cases, event technology platforms will insist on being gatekeepers and owners of that data, which can cause some problems for event experience managers over time. Event technology platforms have a lot to gain by keeping the data for themselves. If, for example, an attendee goes to multiple events in a given year, hosted by multiple organizations, the events technology platform can optimize their experience based on the data it's collected about them from other events. When that same attendee goes to an event that's hosted through a different platform, however, there will be a noticeable difference in their experience, specifically when it comes to personalization and recommendations.

That is why those who are relatively new to the industry, or those organizations with less experience hosting events, often choose to go with a platform that comes with its own trove of data. Rather than building up your data capabilities over time, such platforms provide a high degree of data capability right out of the gate.

While this strategy helps strengthen the power of the platform itself, it can serve to limit many of the other benefits we have outlined regarding data ownership. Namely, event experience managers are more limited in the data they can utilize to make better decisions internally and what they can share with other departments and functions, like sales and marketing.

By contrast, when the event team owns its own data, the data stays with them. That means they are no longer bound to a single platform and have the ability to input their events data freely anywhere they want. It also means that their competitors are not able to utilize the data they collect to offer their attendees a better experience.

When the event team owns its own data, however, it does serve to limit the amount of data they can collect on attendees, from their behavior at every event they attend on one platform to just the events they attend that are run by the same host. As a result, it may take longer to build a rich enough data pool on each attendee to provide a truly personalized experience.

For enterprise or larger event teams, data ownership isn't just an internal debate about platform optimization; it also has security, privacy, and legal implications. Enterprises that choose a platform that retains data ownership rights might ultimately struggle to get approval from other departments, like IT and legal.

In the past, this debate was relatively inconsequential and thus flew under the radar, but as virtual and hybrid events increase the availability of data, it's come into greater focus. Now data ownership is something event experience managers need to take seriously when choosing a technology partner.

Bizzabo, for one, does not own any of the data it collects; all of that attendee data is easily accessible and ready to be utilized for a range of purposes that can help improve internal processes and event strategy moving forward. When it comes to the data ownership debate, we strongly feel that the data should be owned by the organizers and should be used to improve their internal systems and processes, not ours.

Many in the industry share our perspective, but it's important to recognize that there are just as many who don't. We're not necessarily recommending one over the other, though we clearly have a preference. We are, however, encouraging event experience managers to take this ongoing debate into consideration and pursue partnerships with technology providers that are consistent with their data ownership preferences.

Additional Considerations for Enterprise Companies

A few additional factors should be taken into consideration by those hosting large, enterprise-scale events because the needs of a larger organization are often different from those of a small- or medium-sized company, particularly when it comes to event technology.

Enterprises often have a few additional hoops to jump through, a bigger and more international audience to serve, and more opportunities for data integration. Below are a few additional considerations for enterprise customers that are managing a large, global event program.

Customer Success and Customer Support

As discussed earlier, event technology platforms are an extension of the event teams, especially in a more virtual and hybrid environment. Enterprise customers need to understand the level of support they can expect from their technology vendors before making a final decision. Specifically, enterprise customers should ensure that they have a dedicated customer success professional whom they can trust when they need support.

In the best-case scenario, the event platform will even offer support to attendees directly. Any issues attendees run into related to the platform, such as trouble logging in, are solved before having to occupy the time and attention of the event team directly. Not only does this reduce the burden on event staff, but it also ensures timely resolution for individual attendee concerns.

Enterprise customers should also seek out a platform that offers ongoing event consultations, which can help continually optimize their event strategy and capabilities over time. They should also take into consideration the vendor's onboarding process and ensure they have access to a dedicated event success professional who can guide, train, and advise them on how best to use the technology to maximize the experiences they want to create.

Brand Consistency

Event teams that are responsible for orchestrating a global event program should also take into consideration the platform's ability to create a consistent brand experience across its entire events portfolio. Doing so typically requires a high degree of customizability, but the amount of customization can vary between platforms.

Look out for tools that offer the ability to fully customize colors, borders, fonts, backgrounds, cascading style sheets (CSS; a language used for coding websites), and even website layouts to match other brand touch points, and avoid those that insist on displaying their own logo and branding too prominently. Doing so will ensure that attendees recognize the host's brand at each and every touch point and that the event experience remains consistent across the entire events portfolio.

Data Integrations

For many enterprise customers, an event technology platform is only as useful as its ability to integrate with the rest of their tech stack. For example, other teams and departments can't utilize that highly valuable attendee data if the platform isn't compatible with their existing customer relations management (CRM) software and marketing automation platform (MAP).

Native software integrations can facilitate the connection of your event platform to other solutions used across your organization. These include "out of the box" integrations, such as an open application programming interface (API; a flexible method of integration that requires support of technical resources) and an app marketplace (which builds on the flexibility of an open API to provide access to integrations that are easy to install).

The ability to integrate with other software services can help improve the attendee experience through processes like social media integration; streamline ticketing, promotions, and registration through payment processing integrations; and improve internal processes through integrations with workforce management tools.

Data Security and Privacy

Every company needs to consider their data and privacy security policies for just about everything they do these days, but that is especially true of a major event, and even more so for enterprises. When considering an event technology platform, it's important to look into the vendor's compliance certifications for data privacy frameworks, such as Privacy Shield, ISO 27001, and Payment Card Industry Data Security Standard (PCI DSS).

It's also important to ensure that the vendor is compliant with local regulations across all regions in which you operate, such as the General Data Protection Regulation (GDPR) or the California Consumer Privacy Act (CCPA). For added security, consider a vendor's utilization of encryption to help protect attendee data and whether they have a disaster recovery plan to ensure data is protected and recoverable in the event of an emergency.

Permission Controls

A bigger events portfolio often means employing a bigger event team. As most who have worked on a large team know, things can get a little complicated when you have a lot of cooks in the kitchen. When event teams are made up of only a small handful of contributors, the borders between them can often be less defined, but as the size of that team increases, it becomes more important to ensure a clear division of labor.

Consequently, event platforms built for enterprise customers typically offer strong permission controls. Such controls allow event teams to create clear lines of separation and clear levels of responsibility, ensuring that team members have access to all the resources they need, without the ability to unintentionally step on each other's toes.

Stability and Scale

Enterprise clients must also vet prospective event hosting platforms to determine whether they can support the size and scale of their event portfolios. After all, hosting an event for 100,000 people in 100 different countries requires different resources and capabilities than an event for 100 people all living within driving distance of each other.

When considering a technology partner, it's important to ensure that the platform is built for the size and scale that suits your needs. It's also worth looking at testimonials and reviews from other enterprise clients to ensure the platform can handle the load without running the risk of experiencing technical glitches or capacity limitations.

What to Consider When Evaluating a Potential Event Technology Platform

With the rapid expansion of events platforms and with the new opportunities made possible by virtual and hybrid events, event teams will need to consider a broader range of features and capabilities than ever before.

When evaluating an event platform, it's important to understand what's possible, what should be expected, and what key factors should be at the heart of that decision-making process. What follows are several of the most important features and capabilities to consider in the era of hybrid event programs.

Data Ownership Policies

As discussed previously, we believe that it's important for event experience managers to own their own data. We see ourselves as an event service provider, rather than as a data company with an events product. We believe event platforms should serve as an open platform for innovation, much like the Apple App Store or the Google Play Store, providing a framework for others to create and innovate on our platform. Wherever you land in that ongoing debate, it's important to consider data ownership policies as part of your evaluation process.

End-to-End Solution

As the technology that powers event platforms continues to mature, event teams are moving away from relying on point solutions (that is, siloed technologies that solve for a particular event need like a networking app or onsite registration) and toward end-to-end event platforms that offer event teams most, if not all, of the tools and services they need to orchestrate their events in a single technology. These have the flexibility of integrating with an ecosystem of point solutions if needed.

When considering an event platform, ensure that it really can offer all the tools and services you need—from email marketing to content delivery, registration, on-demand content libraries, high-quality streaming, and everything in between. You also want to ensure that your technology partner is committed to ongoing innovation and that they have a proven record of adapting and changing at a pace that suits your business's needs.

Open Platform Design

Event platforms are often only as valuable as the number of other tools and capabilities they can seamlessly interact with. As the inputs and outputs of event platforms grow to encompass a broader range of needs and capabilities, it's important to evaluate the platform's ability to integrate with other tools.

Choosing a provider that features an open platform will allow you to move data easily from the event platform to other services, like your marketing stack and customer relations management software. Open platform solutions, by their nature, also require a robust and solid underlying infrastructure, which can serve as a strong indication of whether the solution is trustworthy.

Create Once, Publish Everywhere (COPE)

The data that you input to your event platform typically exists in a variety of spaces, but it's important that such data remains consistent, no matter where it's found. For example, a speaker's job title might be listed on the home page, the featured speakers' page, within the event agenda builder, on the mobile app, in a banner during the live broadcast, and even on a speaker's badge if they attend in person. Should a speaker's title change in the run-up to an event, as often happens, event experience managers are responsible for changing that information everywhere that it appears.

A create once, publish everywhere (COPE) feature, however, allows event experience managers to make that change once and apply it across the entire platform at once. This is a key feature of a modern content management system (CMS) and can help ensure consistency across the entire digital footprint of the event.

Ease of Use

Event platforms are complicated, but they shouldn't appear that way to end users. When choosing an event platform, it's important to consider whether it's built with an intuitive design that makes it easy to onboard new users and leverage the technology to its full capacity. Being user friendly is a key attribute of an event platform, both for individual team members and for other software platforms and digital services.

Customization

When a user logs onto your event, they should be able to immediately identify the host brand's distinctive features through the colors, fonts, layout, and look and feel. That is why it is important to ensure that your event platform offers a high degree of customization. While the event platform itself will offer all the tools and services you need to orchestrate a successful event, it should also provide the flexibility to utilize those tools in a way that feels authentic to the brand.

Live Support

As event platforms become more complex, and as event teams grow to encompass a wider variety of stakeholders, it's incredibly valuable to choose a platform that offers a high degree of customer support. You should always feel like your technology partner has your back and has dedicated in-house resources ready and waiting to assist you with needs big and small. Having live support at your disposal can also help ensure that you're able to leverage the technology to its fullest potential, enabling you to execute a flawless event.

On-Demand Content Delivery

In a virtual or hybrid environment, content has the opportunity to have a longer and more valuable life cycle than ever before, but only when supported by a strong content library system. Having on-demand content delivery allows your team to repurpose and share event content in a variety of ways that serve a variety of purposes, from follow-up outreach after an event to marketing content for your next event. It also ensures that those who are unable to attend your event live have access to the same content later on.

As a result, you're able to effectively extend the reach of your event and your key messaging well beyond the confines of the event itself. While some event platforms charge extra for on-demand content delivery services, others include it in their base pricing. Either way, it's important to consider how you can leverage that content moving forward and how effective the platform is in enabling you to do so.

Audience Engagement Tools

Engagement is top priority in a virtual and hybrid environment, and your ability to engage an audience will often depend on the tools at your disposal. That is why it's vital to consider how the event platform will facilitate those moments of connection between attendees. While it's hard to feel like part of a community when sitting at home alone in front of a computer screen, the right combination of tools can go a long way toward bringing virtual attendees into the conversation.

Those tools and features include the ability to see who else is attending at a given moment; to filter attendees based on parameters like department, geography, or job title; to view attendee profiles; to have easy access to chat, video conferencing, meeting scheduling; and more. Furthermore, as we move toward more hybrid events, it will be incumbent on the platforms to provide opportunities to bridge the gap between in-person and virtual attendees. Ensuring that your technology partner is focused on attendee engagement is vital in the era of virtual and hybrid events.

Sponsor and Exhibitor Tools

Sponsors and exhibitors have long been the financial engine that drives in-person events, but creating a space for exhibitors and sponsors is far more challenging in a virtual environment. Event platforms have a wide range of solutions that can help ensure those key stakeholders are able to extract value from the event, but some are better at achieving those outcomes than others. Just offering a banner ad or a list of sponsors with links to their websites probably won't cut it.

Before choosing an event platform, it's worth exploring how effective it is at creating value for sponsors and exhibitors. That could include unique sponsorship packages, promotions, sponsored events, live demonstrations, branded meeting rooms, sponsored content, training spaces, and more. What's important is that your technology partner has demonstrated a clear understanding of the needs of your sponsors and exhibitors and can offer tools and features that will make them excited to participate in your events moving forward.

Automation and AI

Artificial intelligence (AI) has become something of a buzzword in the technology industry lately. While just about every start-up and incumbent will boast about their AI capabilities, some are more practical and valuable than others. When used effectively, AI tools should be able to direct attendees to sessions, speakers, and fellow attendees that are most likely to suit their needs and interests.

Providing a higher level of automation can dramatically improve the attendee experience and improve engagement with the event overall. Automation can also help reduce the workload for event teams on the back end, as they can create systems that execute certain commands at the appropriate time. For example, automated email marketing tools can ensure each attendee receives a personalized reminder email before the event, a personalized welcome email at the start of the event, and a personalized follow-up after its conclusion. While just about every software company claims to have the latest AI tools, it's important to evaluate just how practical, robust, and effective they really are.

Data Ownership Policies

As discussed previously, we believe that it's important for event experience managers to own their own data. We see ourselves as an event service provider, rather than as a data company with an events product. We believe event platforms should serve as an open platform for innovation, much like the Apple App Store or the Google Play Store, providing a framework for others to create and innovate on our platform. Wherever you land in that ongoing debate, it's important to consider data ownership policies as part of your evaluation process.

Production Quality

Every event platform now offers the ability to livestream content, but there are many ways to package and present the same information. Ensuring strong, high-definition audio and video is table stakes; event teams should also consider factors like how space can be utilized on screen, such as banners and presentation boards; how polling and surveying tools are integrated into the production; and how effective Q&A sessions are at bringing attendees onto the virtual stage.

Moving forward, event content specialists will need to design their content through the lens of a camera, so it's important to have a technology partner that demonstrates a strong understanding of production quality and broadcasting fundamentals.

Real-Time Event Analytics

Data can help event teams make better, more informed decisions, but in order to do so that data often needs to be readily available and easily accessible in real time. When evaluating an event's success platform, it's important to look for a provider that can capture data points and display them in a way that makes those insights easily understood and actionable. For example, real-time event analytics tools can identify the most viewed and liked attendees, speakers, sponsors, and sessions; capture social media engagement data; and offer insights into the tools and resources attendees are, or aren't, taking advantage of.

With that information, event experience managers can make better decisions about which speakers and subjects to display prominently on their homepage and how to maximize the reach of their social media content. They can also let attendees know which are peak hours for virtual networking. Having real-time analytics will ultimately allow your event team to make more informed decisions and optimize your events in real time.

Stability

Before choosing an event platform, your IT or operations departments will probably want to take a look under the hood. In a more virtual and hybrid future, event professionals should be prepared to work closely with their IT teams to examine a prospective vendor's technical specs, such as streaming quality, load capacity, speed, and reliability. Be sure to consult with your technical stakeholders to ensure the event platform you choose is up to whatever tasks you have planned for it.

What an Event Platform Can (and Can't) Do for You

CHAPTER

What an Event Platform Can
(and Can't) Do for You

Your event platform will be the most important tool in your team's toolbox. But like any tool, it's only as powerful as the people and strategies behind it.

According to Rexson Serrao from Salesforce, in a conversation on the IN-PERSON podcast, "An event technology platform isn't the same thing as an event strategy. That is the number one thing to remember. If your entire strategy says I'm going to use Platform A to deliver the experience, you have a huge problem."

In the past, event technology orbited around an in-person experience. These tools and services helped spread awareness; communicate key messages; and manage ticketing and registration, agendas, and more; but the event still took place in a separate, real-world environment. Some of the tools in the event experience manager toolkit were intended to facilitate an in-person experience, while others were squarely focused on just getting people in the door.

In a virtual or hybrid environment, the event platform is the venue. Just as they do for a physical venue, event experience managers are still responsible for filling a mostly blank space with all of the elements that will allow them to create a unique and memorable experience for attendees.

When shopping for an event platform, it's important to understand the resources that come with it and those you will need to bring to the table yourself. Just as your real-world event venue isn't responsible for designing an experience for your attendees, it's important to similarly see your virtual venue as a blank canvas. Rather than asking your prospective vendors what kind of event their platform is capable of creating, it's far more effective to start with a strategy—including the outcomes you want to drive and the experience you want to facilitate—and look for the platform that can best bring that vision to life.

That is not to say that your strategy can be executed the same regardless of the platform you choose; some will offer tools and resources that will better help you achieve those outcomes than others. It is important to recognize, however, that a good strategy with a clear definition of goals and outcomes is often more consequential than the platform itself.

In some cases that might require rethinking your agency partnerships as well. Those that have operated in the events industry for a long time likely have long-standing relationships with their agency of choice, but as you pivot toward more virtual and hybrid events, it's important to find an agency partner that can pivot with you. In some cases, that will lead to some difficult decisions, but at the end of the day results should come before relationships.

As Melissa Patruno, executive producer at the event management agency Bishop-McCann, shared with us recently at an agency roundtable discussion in April 2021, "We talk a lot about agencies being platform agnostic. While Bishop-McCann still holds that statement to be true for us—we do work in many different platforms dependent upon what the client is looking for—as an agency, clients are also looking to us to be able to make recommendations and to let them know we've done our research."

It's important to recognize that an event expert in the in-person era might not have the necessary skills to utilize your event platform to its fullest capacity. As an event professional you will want to ensure that you're working with subject matter experts who have experience utilizing the platform you choose, even if it means changing agencies.

The transition from an in-person venue to a virtual venue also requires event experience managers to be more thoughtful about their attendees' basic needs. Just as a physical venue provides access to things like bathrooms, food vendors, water fountains, outdoor spaces, and other elements that serve our basic human functions, it's important to build human elements into your virtual event strategy as well. At the end of the day, attendees are not customers, they're not prospects, they're not even attendees—they're humans. This is where inclusion and accessibility really come into play. In the hybrid era, successful events will be those that create an environment that all attendees can participate in.

As Sean Doyle, the event marketing lead at Pinterest, mentioned in an episode of the IN-PERSON podcast published in May 2021:

> I think when it comes to hybrid, we can't just rely on this digital, this virtual element, being the answer to accessibility. We need to make sure the experiences we create, the venues that we choose, and the way we design our spaces and production continue to be accessible for as many people as possible—otherwise you're not really being fully inclusive, you're just providing an alternative, rather than actually including people.

While the new team roles that we discussed in Part 4 will be key to producing hybrid experiences that are not just approachable, but welcoming, we also believe it's important to bring in some outside experts as well—namely, your target audience.

Devin Cleary, Bizzabo's vice president of global events, is passionate on this topic (and we don't blame him):

> Bring your customers in, create a focus group, create a steering committee, vet all of it with individuals who are your attendees or your ICP [ideal customer profile],

and let them validate for you if you're hitting the mark. You usually have thousands of people at your disposal— especially if we're talking about a flagship event—that are going to happily give you their opinions, or validate something that you're trying to test out . . . and they're going to be very receptive to that kind of opportunity, to make sure you're delivering what they expect.

Event platforms can help event experience leaders accomplish a lot of truly incredible things, but at the end of the day it's just a tool, and tools are only as useful as the people and strategies behind them. While it's important to spend the necessary time and resources vetting, testing, and ultimately onboarding an event platform, you can't expect it to solve all of your problems or give you all of the right answers.

When it comes to crafting and delivering a successful event program, there's only so much event technology can do. At the end of the day, a successful event program requires a strong strategy, a clear understanding of goals and key outcomes, and a team that can utilize the software to its full potential in order to facilitate a truly unique and enjoyable experience for attendees.

Taking on the Future of Experiences

At the time of this writing, it's hard to blame anyone for feeling uncertain about the future, both within the events industry and beyond. Some venues have begun reopening—most under some health and safety restrictions—and there is both excitement and hesitation to return to in-person events.

Many people are eagerly anticipating attending their next major in-person event; however, a sizable proportion of the population isn't as ready to return to in-person venues just yet, if ever. Whether for health and safety reasons, disability, social anxiety, limited budgets, or limited schedule availability, there will remain a significant number of attendees who prefer the virtual format in the months and years ahead.

That is why, despite the regular use of the word *hybrid* throughout this book, we believe the term *hybrid events* will gradually fade into history. Moving forward, most event playbooks will need to include some virtual elements in order to maximize their potential, to remain inclusive, and to provide attendees with options that suit their needs. Much in the same way that we no longer refer to using our phones to make purchases and transactions as *online banking*, hybrid events won't need their own moniker because they will quickly become the standard. To that same end, hybrid strategy will just become the default way to view, and plan for, the ongoing hybrid spectrum of events.

We've spent much of this book talking about the more distant future, but here we'd like to share a few thoughts on the state of events as they exist today and what it will take to host a safe and successful event in the immediate future. If you're reading this in a world where COVID-19 restrictions are a relic of the past, consider the following a history lesson. If health and safety protocols are still of concern, however, we hope this will be of assistance.

The Immediate Future of Events

Much about the immediate future of events remains unknown. Between vaccine hesitancy and new, more contagious coronavirus variants, social distancing requirements, and travel restrictions, it's hard to say exactly when event participation will feel the same as it once did. In the interim, there are a few new factors that event teams will need to consider as they begin a gradual return to the in-person venue.

Venue Considerations

Looking for a venue during this unique period in our industry's history requires some additional considerations. For example, in-person venues simply cannot accommodate the same number of people at a time where social distancing is still a priority. When looking for a venue, it's important to find a space that has lots of breathing room, not only on the exhibition floor and keynote stages, but in lounge areas and common spaces as well. Venues and municipalities might also have their own gathering restrictions, so be sure to ask about their limitations.

As you negotiate venue contracts in this new environment, a few elements should be top of mind. Cancellation, postponement, and liability policies should be taken into greater consideration, as well as "force majeure," a clause that relieves all parties of any responsibility in the event of uncontrollable circumstances. Finally, it's also a good idea to secure venue insurance to cover you in case of an unexpected problem that requires you to postpone or cancel your event. In this highly uncertain period, there really is no such thing as a guarantee.

Health and Safety Measures

There are a number of health and safety precautions that organizers will have to consider to ensure their flagship doesn't unintentionally become a super-spreader event. Requiring proof of a negative COVID test or a vaccination will likely be part of the check-in process, as well as onsite health screenings, in addition to more traditional security checks. Despite these restrictions and requirements, event experience managers are still responsible for offering a stellar in-person experience, even as attendees are required to jump through these hurdles.

While some countries and states have dropped their mask mandates, masks remain one of the best ways to prevent unintentional viral spread, especially among a large crowd. Requiring masks and providing access to personal protective equipment (PPE) onsite are important precautionary steps. Fortunately, masks and other PPE provide a branding opportunity; you can create custom branded masks with your logo, or your sponsor's logo, to publicize brands within the venue and beyond, especially if they're reusable.

Sanitization stations are also likely to be a standard site at events for the foreseeable future, and it's important to promote strong hygiene practices by making hand sanitizer readily available throughout the venue. Strategists should also seek to offer a contactless experience that limits the number of surfaces and items that attendees need to physically touch in order to attend your event. Mobile tickets, contactless payments, and onsite badge printing improve not only safety, but also convenience.

When it comes to food and beverage, buffets are generally not recommended, but if you do wish to provide a buffet, make sure there are sneeze guards in place and that the only people who come into direct contact with food are designated servers in full PPE. As an alternative, consider providing a grab-and-go or prepackaged box meal that attendees can take with them. Outdoor seating, especially for meals and snacks, is also recommended whenever possible.

All of these changes are likely to require additional consideration and additional budget allocation. As you map out your costs, it's important not only to include the health and safety protocols you prepare for in advance, but also to factor in some additional flexibility in case additional measures or precautions are necessary.

Communication

Whatever health and safety precautions you put in place, make sure you communicate those procedures to your attendees, both before and during the event. It's important to recognize that this is a traumatic time for many, and attendees will require a high degree of sensitivity and understanding in order to feel comfortable at your event. Using ample signage and distributing safety guides can help ensure your guests understand what precautions are being taken and how to abide by the necessary health and safety measures you've put in place.

At a time where many attendees remain skittish about the return to large in-person gatherings, it's important to keep them in the loop well before the event kicks off. Clearly and prominently explaining the health and safety measures you've put into place will help increase their confidence in attending in person. It's similarly important to make virtual options clear, providing an opportunity for those who might still be hesitant to participate remotely.

Experience Design Still Counts

All of these health and safety protocols have the potential to significantly disrupt the attendee experience, but event experience managers are still responsible for delivering a stellar experience. If your health and safety measures are too overbearing, or create too much of a burden on attendees, they might hesitate to attend in-person events in the future.

That is why it's important to ensure you have enough staff on hand to administer safety checks and facilitate a smooth check-in experience, as an example. Attendees ultimately want to feel safe, but not overburdened by health and safety measures. It's a difficult balance to strike, but one that event experience managers will have to consider as they design their in-person experiences in the COVID-19 era.

General Best Practices

Beyond those more tangible health and safety measures, event teams operating under these new circumstances will need to develop a few new skills and habits. For example, it's important to remain adaptable and flexible, given the number of unknowns that remain. Understand that agility is a necessary skill in this uncertain environment and that there's only so much within your control.

It's similarly important to have a backup plan, or multiple contingency plans, that will allow you to react to unforeseen circumstances quickly and effectively. Furthermore, it's important to remain on top of recommendations from the CDC (Centers for Disease Control) and WHO (World Health Organization) and ensure that you're abiding by best practices based on the most recent data available from reputable sources.

This Is Our Moment

You might be feeling a little discouraged about the state of our industry, but for most event experience managers there really is a lot to be excited about.

Despite ongoing health and safety concerns, we believe there has never been a more exciting time to be part of this industry; to have a hand in shaping what is quickly becoming the most important marketing channel in a company's toolbox; to experiment with new formats and technologies; to reimagine the event experience from the ground up. The revolution of events is upon us, and we are all active participants in writing its history.

The industry as a whole has made incredible progress since the start of the pandemic, but we're really only just scratching the surface of what's possible. In the coming years, we'll continue to find new and innovative ways to improve the attendee experience, to push the boundaries of the imagination, and to unleash the full potential of professional events.

This is a transformational period that will ultimately serve to give the industry the technology upgrade it has long resisted, to leverage data to improve the attendee experience, and to elevate events—and their staff—within the enterprise at large.

And we're just getting started. In the coming years, new tools, trends, and technologies will further enable events to reach new heights. They will enable new business models and facilitate even greater value for event stakeholders. Emerging technologies like virtual and augmented reality, artificial intelligence, big data processing, and the Internet will continually improve the event experience in the years to come.

The rise of remote and hybrid work is already reshaping our world in profound ways. As the technology industry focuses more intentionally on providing better remote experiences, the opportunities for event experience managers will continue to grow. We imagine a future of events that exist as a yearlong community, in which participants interact with their industry and its thought leaders on an ongoing basis, with regular events serving as touch points along the way.

The events industry has existed relatively unchanged for generations; now we're in a period of rapid innovation, and the possibilities are seemingly endless. While the immediate future is full of unknowns, we can confidently say that the long-term outlook for event professionals and the events industry as a whole is very bright and full of potential.

One of the most valuable lessons we've learned throughout the pandemic period was the need to constantly evolve, and now we have the tools and the skills to embrace whatever innovation lies ahead. Another major lesson has been the value of sharing best practices and coming together as a community to solve our most pressing challenges. We hope to continue sharing those lessons and best practices with you at a future event, whether virtual, in-person, or somewhere in between.

References

Alexa. 2021. "Top Sites." Alexa.com. https://www.alexa.com/topsites.

Bennett, Lindsay. 2018. "Marketers Still Lagging as Consumers Shift to Vertical Video." *AdNews*, August 2. https://www.adnews.com.au/news/marketers-still-lagging-as-consumers-shift-to-vertical-video.

Bertoni, Steven. 2021. "Exclusive: Harry's Raises a $155 Million Series E at $1.7 Billion, A Year After the FTC Blocked Its Billion-Dollar Sale to Edgewell." *Forbes*, March 31. forbes.com/sites/stevenbertoni/2021/03/31/exclusive-harrys-raises-a-155-million-series-e--at-17-billion-a-year-after-the-ftc-blocked-its-billion-dollar-sale-to-edgewell/?sh=cd1f3fa97593.

Bizbash Editors. 2019. "See Who Won the 2019 BizBash Event Style Awards." Bizbash.com, October 23. https://www.bizbash.com/catering-design/media-gallery/21091956/2019-bizbash-event-style-awards-winners-list.

Bizzabo. 2019. *IN-PERSON: The Power of Human Connection*. https://welcome.bizzabo.com/ebooks/in-person-collection.

Bizzabo. 2019. "2020 Event Marketing Report." https://welcome.bizzabo.com/reports/event-marketing-2020.

Bizzabo. 2020. *Evolution of Events Report*. https://welcome.bizzabo.com/reports/evolution-of-events-report.

Bizzabo.2020. "How DataRobot Launched a Worldwide Virtual Event Series with Bizzabo." https://www.bizzabo.com/resources/cases-studies/datarobot.

Bizzabo. 2021. *The Virtual Attendee Experience Report.* https://welcome .bizzabo.com/reports/virtual-attendee-experience-report.

Bizzabo. 2021. *The Virtual Event Benchmarks Report: Q2 2021.* https:// welcome.bizzabo.com/virtual-events-benchmarks.

Bizzabo. n.d. "The IN-PERSON Podcast." https://blog.bizzabo.com/ in-person-podcast.

Bouwer, Jaap, Steve Saxon, and Nina Wittkamp. 2021. "Back to the future? Airline sector poised for change post-COVID-19." *McKinsey & Company*, (April). mckinsey.com/industries/travel-logistics-and-infrastructure/our-insights/back-to-the-future-airline-sector-poised-for-change-post-covid-19.

Business Model Navigator. n.d. Accessed September 13, 2021. https:// businessmodelnavigator.com/case-firm?id=8.

CareerBuilder. 2014. "Overwhelming Majority of Companies Say Soft Skills Are Just as Important as Hard Skills." April 10. https:// press.careerbuilder.com/2014-04-10-Overwhelming-Majority-of-Companies-Say-Soft-Skills-Are-Just-as-Important-as-Hard-Skills-According-to-a-New-CareerBuilder-Survey.

CNBC Make It Staff. 2019. "This CEO sold his company for $1 billion—here's how he finds work-life balance." CNBC.com, February 6.

Cook, Karla. 2016. "A Brief History of Online Advertising." HubSpot .com. blog.hubspot.com/marketing/history-of-online-advertising.

Crook, Jordan. 2020. "Warby Parker, valued at $3 billion, raises $245 million in funding." TechCrunch, August 27. techcrunch.com/ 2020/08/27/warby-parker-valued-at-3-billion-raises-245-million-in-funding/.

Demandbase. 2021. 2021 ABM Benchmark Study. https://www.demand-base.com/ebook/2021-abm-benchmark-study-measurement/.

Dixon, Ed. 2020. "2020 LoL World Championship draws 3.8m peak viewers." Sportspromedia, November 5. https://www.sportspromedia .com/news/league-of-legends-world-championship-2020-final-audience-viewing-figures/.

Fitch, Adam. 2020. "Why brands like Spotify & Louis Vuitton advertise through League of Legends." Dexerto, October 30. https://www.dexerto.com/business/league-of-legends-worlds-partnerships-1443183/.

Fortune. n.d. "SAP Company Profile." Accessed September 13, 2021. https://fortune.com/company/sap/global500/.

Jeffries, Adrianne. 2012. "Reddit has its biggest day ever thanks to President Obama's AMA." *The Verge*, August 29. https://www.theverge.com/2012/8/29/3277766/president-obamas-ama-most-popular-post-on-reddit-ever.

Mann, Charles Riborg. 1918. *A Study of Engineering Education*. Carnegie Foundation.

Patel, Sahil. 2016. "85 percent of Facebook video is watched without sound." DigiDay, May 17. https://digiday.com/media/silent-world-facebook-video/.

Peters, Brian. 2019. "Does Vertical Video Make a Difference? We Spent $6,000 on Tests to Find Out." Buffer, February 19. https://buffer.com/resources/vertical-video/.

Russell, Michelle. 2020. "What Skills Will Event Professionals Need in the COVID-19 Recovery?" PCMA, April 30. https://www.pcma.org/job-skills-event-professionals-covid-19-recovery/.

SAP. n.d. "About SAP." Accessed September 13, 2021. https://www.sap.com/about/company.html.

"(SAP) valuation MEASURES & financial statistics." n.d. Yahoo! Finance. Accessed September 12, 2021. https://finance.yahoo.com/quote/SAP/key-statistics.

Savage, Chris. 2018. "Introducing One, Ten, One Hundred—A Wistia Original Series." Wistia, September 24. https://wistia.com/learn/show-news/introducing-one-ten-one-hundred.

Szewczyk, Tod. 2021. "A Field Guide to Virtual Event Platforms: Chapter 2—Virtual Experience Platforms." August Jackson, January 21. https://www.augustjackson.com/a-field-guide-to-virtual-event-platforms-chapter-2-virtual-experience-platforms/.

Vig, Himanshu, and Roshan Deshmukh. 2021. "Events Industry by Type (Music Concert, Festivals, Sports, Exhibitions & Conferences, Corporate Events & Seminars, and Others), Revenue Source (Ticket Sale, Sponsorship, and Others), Organizer (Corporate, Sports, Education, Entertainment, and Others)." Allied Market Research.

VSef. n.d. Accessed September 22, 2021. https://vsef.io/welcome.

Whitten, Sarah. 2020. "'Schitt's Creek' has record-setting Emmy sweep, while HBO scores big with 'Watchmen,' 'Succession.'" CNBC, September 20. https://www.cnbc.com/2020/09/20/emmys-2020-the-complete-list-of-winners-and-nominees.html.

Wright, Joe. 2018. "The origin of soft skills." JoeJag: Just Another Dev, February 17. https://code.joejag.com/2018/the-origin-of-soft-skills.html.

Acknowledgments

When we set out to write this book at the end of 2020, we were thrilled to explore the future of the industry but were also still in shock. Event professionals had done it; we'd done it: Somehow we as an industry had managed to get through one of the most difficult professional and personal years of our lives. We had seen first-hand the toll taken on our customers, our employees, and our peers. We had seen event leaders lose headcount and budget when in-person events were canceled at the beginning of the year and then fight tooth-and-claw battles to prove the value of their programs in a virtual and hybrid world.

If we're being honest, we also saw event technology companies like ours implode from a dwindling customer base or simply not innovating quickly enough to meet the demands of an unprecedented event landscape. And while we were proud that Bizzabo had weathered the transition to a hybrid world so well, we felt a bit of survivor's guilt for the companies, the teams, the vendors, and the event professionals who didn't.

Writing this book—speaking to our friends in the industry, consulting with our team members, squeezing in time amid the hustle of C-suite life to talk through a chapter, a datapoint, a trend—was a kind of therapy. It was a process of reminding ourselves of just how much opportunity there is and will be in this industry we call professional events.

With that said, we owe our most sincere thanks to Nicola Kastner, Colleen Bisconti, Monique Ruff-Bell, Dana Pake, Orson Francescone, and Marco Giberti for generously giving their time for conversations throughout the writing of this book. We'd also like to thank the 50-plus guests from the IN-PERSON Podcast whose conversations were an invaluable reference. A special thanks to Rexson Serrao, Sean Doyle, and Andrea Long, whose words we reference in these pages. We consider ourselves extremely lucky to have the opportunity to consult the perspectives of these event experience leaders.

Of course, without our customers we would not have been able to get to this point to begin with. Thanks for believing in us when things were at their roughest and trusting us to be partners with you all as we navigate the exciting (and sometimes nerve-wracking) future of the industry.

And we could say the same of our Bizzaboers. The past two years have been challenging. But through it all you have been our rock. We mean it. In the face of so many challenges, you have driven the company forward so that we can better serve our industry and the human beings in it who depend on us for their events and their jobs. And you've done it all like Bizzaboers do: with compassion for fellow team members, empathy for our customers, a high bar for excellence, and a willingness to try out new ideas and to share your own with us.

We are also extremely grateful for the support of our investors who believed in us in our early days and those who have participated in more recent funding rounds. Thank you for pushing us and for dreaming with us. We are only getting started.

Thank you also to Jared Lindzon, Michelle Bruno, and Mike Sholars for their assistance in bringing this book to life. And a special thanks to the one and only Brandon Rafalson—a true

Bizzaboer whose dedication and thought leadership made this book possible.

We can't help but also squeeze in a few more very important thank-yous: To our amazing wives (Tal, Tal, and Sivan), who provide us with unconditional and endless support, and to all of the many kids—thank you for adding so much joy to our life.

About Bizzabo

Bizzabo powers immersive in-person, virtual, and hybrid experiences. The Bizzabo Event Experience OS is a data-rich open platform that allows event experience leaders to manage events, engage audiences, activate communities, and deliver powerful business outcomes—all while keeping attendee data private and secure. As a leader in The Forrester Wave™: B2B Marketing Events Management Solutions, Q1 2021 Report, we are trusted by world-leading brands to power their events, from Fortune 100 enterprise organizations and financial institutions to creative agencies and scaling tech companies. Bizzabo was founded by Alon Alroy, Eran Ben-Shushan, and Boaz Katz and has hundreds of employees in its New York, Tel-Aviv, Kyiv, Montreal, and London offices, as well as dozens of remote locations around the world. You can learn more about the company, its technology, and open careers at Bizzabo.com.

About the Authors

Alon, Eran, and Boaz co-founded Bizzabo in 2011. The three met at the prestigious Zell Entrepreneurship program at Reichman University in Israel. After attending numerous professional events while working on a separate start-up idea, they saw an opportunity to build a new way to bring attendees together. After months of working out of a family garage, they realized connecting attendees was just the beginning. The real opportunity was to connect every aspect of the event experience.

Alon Alroy

Alon is co-founder, chief marketing officer, and chief customer officer at Bizzabo. Soon after founding Bizzabo, Alon emerged as an important voice within the event industry. He was recognized as a "40 Under 40 Young Leaders" by *Collaborate Magazine*, "100 Most Influential People in the Event Industry" by Eventex, and one of the Top 10 Israeli CMOs by *Geektime* magazine.

Alon began his career in the Israeli Air Force, where he served as a special forces team commander for six years. Prior to founding Bizzabo, he was a senior start-ups analyst at ISP Financials. He graduated with high honors from Reichman University, where he earned his BA in business and LLB in law. He was selected to participate in the prestigious Zell Entrepreneurship Program and in New York's exclusive Venture Fellows Program.

Alon is based out of New York City with his wife, kids, and Jack Russell Terrier (and unofficial Bizzabo mascot), Vee. He can frequently be seen beating Eran in Ping-Pong.

Eran Ben-Shushan

Eran is co-founder and CEO of Bizzabo. From his earliest days in the events industry to his time at Bizzabo, Eran has been passionate about bringing people together and making events more human. With this approach in mind, he led the growth of Bizzabo's team from three co-founders with a dream to hundreds of employees and one of the most successful event technology companies in the world. Eran has been named one of "2021's Most Influential Event Professionals" by BizBash and has been featured in the *Software Report*'s Top 50 SaaS CEOs for three years.

Eran began his career in the Israeli Air Force, serving as an officer for nine years. He then served as the CEO of the Rosh-Pina Media Convention, one of the largest annual professional events in Israel. He was also a team leader and systems engineer at Elbit Systems. Eran graduated cum laude from Reichman University, where he studied business and participated in the prestigious Zell Entrepreneurship Program.

Eran lives in New York City with his wife and kids. Despite what Alon may say, Eran can in fact frequently be seen beating him in Ping-Pong.

Boaz Katz

Boaz is co-founder and chief data officer at Bizzabo. Throughout his career, Boaz has been obsessed with two things: building innovative products and data. At Bizzabo, Boaz channels this unique perspective through the company's data-driven product strategy and by equipping Bizzabo's customers with original insights surfaced from the Bizzabo platform.

Prior to Bizzabo, Boaz designed airborne interfaces for helicopters with Lockheed Martin and Sikorsky for three years while serving in the Israeli Air Force. After this, he continued to spearhead innovative products as the lead product manager at Elbit Systems. Boaz graduated from Reichman University, where he studied for a BA in computer science and participated in the prestigious Zell Entrepreneurship Program.

Boaz lives in Israel. When he's not working or surfing, he can be seen leading cooking classes for his kids (and his fellow Bizzaboers) and serving the resulting dishes to his wife.

Index

Account-based marketing (ABM)
  communication skills and, 167
  defined, 57–58
  events and, 68
  at SAP, 66
  understanding, 152
Active listening, 167
Adaptability, 165
Advertising, digital, 53–54
Airbnb, 39, 41
AirWorks conference, 56
Almost IN-PERSON, 19, 20, 29
Amazon, 9, 19, 39, 41, 50, 153
Amazon Career Day, 153
Apple, 9, 39, 75, 154
Application programming interface
  (API), 210
Arnaz, Desi, 83
Artificial intelligence (AI),
  49–50, 194, 217
Attendee data
  protecting, 73–74, 210–211
  silos of, 75–76
  trusted organizers and, 74–75
Attendee experience, 42–44
Attendees
  best experience of, 49
  communication with, 58–59
  tailored agenda for, 48–49

Audience, reaching the right
  digital advertising as example of,
    53–55
  post-event communications, 58–59
  registration patterns, 55–57
  targeting key accounts, 57–58
Audience development/event
  marketer, 185
Audience engagement. *See also*
  Engagement principles
  Event Impact Gap and, 28, 30–31
  tools, 215–216

Benchmarks, reliance on, 10
Bieber, Justin, 182
Bisconti, Colleen, 6, 20, 21, 22, 23, 108,
  109, 111, 112, 121,
  141, 151, 155
Bishop-McCann agency, 224
BizBash Event Style Award, 65
Bizzabo, 18, 27, 41, 56, 64, 166, 172, 175,
  184, 191, 194, 195,
  207, 225, 245
Blair, Tony, 119
Business travel, future of, 82

California Consumer Privacy Act
  (CCPA), 210
Camaraderie, facilitating, 7

Camera and sound operators, 182–183
Can't-miss shared experiences, 121–123
Cannes-Lions, 32, 150
Career path. *See also* Skills for event
    experience managers
    diversity of skills, 171–175
    relevant experience, 175–176
CareerBuilder, 160
Change
    permanent, 11–12
    resistance to, 7–9
Christophe-Garcia, Chardia, 5–6
Cisco, 9, 87, 194
Cleary, Devin, 41–42, 43, 75, 166–167,
    175–176, 181–182,
    185, 186, 225
Collaboration skills, 13, 167–168
Communication skills, 32, 165–168
Community building
    can't-miss shared experiences,
      121–123
    eSports industry and, 87
    hybrid environments and, 83
    importance of, 86–87, 117
    marketing efforts and, 121
    through virtual events, 118–120
Content
    engaging, 86
    importance of, 85–86
    interactivity, 109–111
    as key to engagement, 105
    medium to complement message,
      111–112
    on-demand, 112–113, 215
    personalization for, 107–109
    production value, 109
    virtual attendee personas
      and, 106–107
Cost per mille (CPM), 54
Covid-19 era
    advantages of virtual events, 18
    challenges of, 17–18
    digital by default, 22–23

    early case study, 18–20
    health and safety measures, 231–233
    impact on event industry, 11–12
    transition to online format, 20–22
Create Once, Publish Everywhere
    (COPE), 213–214
Customer success manager, 186
Cyberattacks, 75

Daniel, J. Damany, 82
Data, and Event Impact Gap, 28, 29–30
Data breaches, 75
Data capture, 47
Data integration, 47–48, 209–210
Data ownership debate, 205–208, 212
Data proliferation, 65
Data security and privacy, 210–211
Data silos, 75–76
Data translation, 48–49
DataRobot, 44
Delayed events, 84
Demandbase, 58
Digital advertising, 53–54
Digital content production, 154–155
Digital-first forever, 120
Disruption, technological
    age of, 39
    attendee experience and, 42–44
    benefits of digital transformation, 44
    data collection and, 41–42, 44
    mass personalization and, 40–41
Diverse workforce, 65
Diversity and inclusion, 143–144
Diversity of skills, 171–175
DJI drone company, 56–57
Dollar Shave Club, 40
DoubleClick advertising agency, 54
Doyle, Sean, 225

Early bird pricing, 55–56
Economic value of event industry, 9
Emmy Awards, 2020, 133
Emotional Intelligence, 160

Emotional intelligence, defined,160
Empathy, 13, 163
Empowered customers, 65
Engagement principles
    community, 83, 86–87
    content, 83, 85–86, 105
    experience design, 83, 87–88
    format, 83–85
    for hybrid world, 82–83
Enterprise resource planning (ERP)
        systems, 64
eSports events, 87
European Union's General Data
        Protection Regulation
        (GDPR), 73, 74
Event data maturity curve
    data capture, 47
    data integration, 47–48
    data utilization, 47, 48
    defined, 47
    insights, 48–49
    outcomes and, 49–50
Event experience leader, 67
Event experience managers. See also
        Skills for event experience
        managers
    age of, 140
    diversity, inclusion, and, 143–144
    elevating role of, 144–145
    Event Impact Gap and, 28
    future of, 141–142
    nontraditional backgrounds of, 142
    skills for, 12–13, 31–32, 141–142,
        171–175
    transition to, 140–141
Event Impact Gap
    audience engagement, 28, 30–31
    data, 28, 29–30
    defined, 27–28
    people and process, 28, 31–32
    technology, 28, 32–33, 195
Event industry
    disruption to, 9–11

    economic value of, 9
    history of inertia, 7–9
    pandemic's impact on, 11–12
    three key themes for, 12–14
Event platforms
    evaluating, 212–219
    what they can and can't do, 223–226
Event strategists, 139–140
Event strategy
    registration data and, 55–57
    return on investment (ROI) and, 55
Event team of the future
    hybrid events team, 185–186
    in-person event team, 183–185
    virtual events team, 180–183
Event technologist, 180–181
Event technology, importance of,
        195–196
Event technology providers. See also
        Technology partners/vendors
    changing landscape for, 191
    expansion and consolidation
        of, 192–195
EventNerd, The, 82
Events, importance of, 5–7
Exclusivity, 99
Executive producer, 181–182
Experience design
    challenges of, 127
    defined, 87–88
    humanizing events, 133–134
    hybrid environment and, 83
    NBA bubble example, 83, 87,
        88, 110, 131
    outcome-based design, 130
    personality types and, 128–129
    personalizing the experience,
        129–130
    sharing the experience, 131–132
    user experience, 130–131
    wow factor, 132–133
Experience Seeker, 106
Eyewear industry, 40

Facebook, 50
Field marketing, defined, 58
Financial Times, 117, 118
FOMO (fear of missing out), 97
Forbes, 185
Format, event
    four hybrid models for, 84
    hybrid events, 100–102
    in-person events, 96–99
    spectrum of options for, 83
    understanding value of, 85
    virtual events, 93–96
Forrest, Hugh, 6
Francescone, Orson, 21, 22, 23, 117, 118,
    119–120, 141, 143
FT Live, 21, 23, 117, 119–120, 143

General Data Protection Regulation
    (GDPR), 73, 74
Giberti, Marco, 8, 9, 43–44, 73, 76
GitHub, 32, 141, 165
Global Boardroom virtual event, 21, 119
Goleman, Daniel, 160
Google, 9, 75
Graziano, Joey, 109

Harry's (subscription service), 40, 44
Health and safety measures, 231–233
Hotel industry, 39
HotWired website, 53
HubSpot, 41, 185, 193
Human connection, 6, 81. *See also*
    Engagement principles
Human resources, 153
Hybrid events
    advantages of, 100
    best practices, 101–102
    best used for, 100–101
    disadvantages of, 100
    engagement at, 82–83
    less effective for, 101
Hybrid events team
    audience development/event
        marketer, 185
    event experience manager, 186

I Love Lucy, 83–84
IBM, 9, 20, 23, 32, 63, 108, 141,
    151, 155
Inclusion and diversity, 143–144
In-person event team
    moderator, 183–184
    onsite technician, 184–185
In-person events
    advantages of, 96
    best practices, 98–99
    best used for, 97
    disadvantages of, 96–97
    less effective for, 98
Insights, from data, 48–49
Internal Socializer, 106

Karamat, Sherrif, 139
Kashi, Keyana, 182
Kastner, Nicola, 23, 42, 48, 63–69, 86
Key accounts, targeting, 57–58
Key performance indicators
    (KPIs), 153

League of Legends World
    Championship, 2020, 87
Linendoll, Katie, 184
Live studio audiences, 83–84
Long, Andrea, 144
Loopd, 192

Managers, event experience. *See also*
    Skills for event experience
    managers
    age of, 140
    diversity, inclusion, and, 143–144
    elevating role of, 144–145
    Event Impact Gap and, 28
    future of, 141–142
    nontraditional backgrounds of, 142
    skills for, 12–13, 31–32, 141–142,
        171–175
    transition to, 140–141
Mandated Learners, 106, 107
Mann, Charles Riborg, 159, 160
Marketo, 193

Mass personalization, 40–41
Mayer, John D., 160
McKenna, Lindsay Niemic, 6
Mercedes-Benz, 87
Microsoft, 9
Microsoft Teams, 193
Model disruption, 65
Moderator, 183–184
Money 20/20, 32, 150

NBA bubble, 83, 87, 88, 110, 131
Net Promoter Score (NPS), 9–10
Netflix, 39, 41, 44, 50, 82, 113, 129

Obama, Barack, 88, 123
On-demand content, 112–113, 215
Onsite technician, 184–185

Pake, Dana, 141, 143, 145, 150, 151, 163,
    164–165, 179, 180–181
Pandemic, impact of, 11–12. *See also*
    Covid-19 era
Patruno, Melissa, 224
Payment Card Industry Data Security
    Standard (PCI DSS), 210
People and process, 28, 31–32
Personal protective equipment (PPE),
    231, 232
Personalization, mass, 40–41
Pinterest, 225
Post-event communications, 58–59
Privacy and security, data, 73–74,
    210–211
Problem solving skills, 163–164
Professional Convention Management
    Association (PCMA),
    139, 162
Professional path. *See also* Skills for event
    experience managers
    diversity of skills, 171–175
    relevant experience, 175–176
Public relations, 154
Purpose of in-person events, 98

Q&A function, 204, 218

Radical Networker, 106, 128
Real-time event analytics, 218
Reddit, 122–123
Registration data, using, 55–57
Request for proposal (RFP)
    process, 205
Resource scarcity, 65
Return on events (ROE)
    data and, 30
    defined, 10
    engagement and, 13
    measuring, 10, 12, 14, 44
    qualitative metrics and, 14
Return on investment (ROI)
    digital advertising and, 54
    event strategy and, 55–57
Ruff-Bell, Monique, 150, 152, 162–163,
    168, 172–175

Sales and marketing, 152–153
Salesforce, 9, 19, 29, 40, 95, 96, 185,
    193, 223
Salovey, Peter, 160
SAP, 63, 66, 67
SAPPHIRE NOW, 63, 64–65, 67,
    68, 86
Serrao, Rexson, 29, 40–41, 95,
    96, 180, 223
Shaffer, Nani, 58
Short virtual experiences, 95
Skills for event experience managers
    data and technology, 149–151
    digital content production,
        154–155
    human resources, 153
    new, 31–32, 141–142
    public relations, 154
    sales and marketing, 152–153
    soft, 13, 159–168
    tech industry design principles,
        151–152
Soft skills
    active listening, 167
    adaptability, 165
    brief history of, 159–161

Soft skills (*Continued*)
  collaboration skills, 13, 167–168
  communication skills, 165–168
  defined, 142, 159
  empathy, 13, 163
  managing uncertainty, 164–165
  pandemic period and, 161–162
  problem solving, 163–164
Solo Learners, 106
Speaker-only events, 84
Sponsor and exhibitor tools, 216
Spotify, 39, 41, 87, 182
Stakeholders and committees,
    202–203
Statement of work (SOW), 203
Strategic Networker, 106, 128
Subscription services, 40

Teams, event
  hybrid events team, 185–186
  in-person event team, 183–185
  virtual events team, 180–183
Tech industry design principles,
    151–152
Technological disruption
  age of, 39
  attendee experience and, 42–44
  benefits of digital transformation, 44
  data collection and, 41–42, 44
  mass personalization and, 40–41
Technology, and Event Impact
    Gap, 28, 32–33
Technology literacy, 149–151
Technology partners/vendors
  attendee experience and, 203–205
  changing landscape for, 191
  data ownership debate, 205–208
  enterprise-scale events and,
    208–211
  evaluating event platforms,
    212–219
  expansion and consolidation
    of, 192–195

questions to ask yourself, 199–202
  stakeholders, committees,
    and, 202–203
TeeVid, 195
Think 2021, 108
TikTok, 155
Twilio, 144
Twitter, 19

Uncertainty, managing, 164–165
Unilever, 40
User data
  data ownership debate, 205–208, 212
  protecting, 73–74, 210–211
  silos of, 75–76
  trusted organizers and, 74–75
User experience, 130–131

Vendors, technology. *See* Technology
    partners/vendors
Venue considerations, 230–231
Virtual events
  advantages of, 18, 93–94
  best practices, 95–96
  best used for, 94
  building community
    through, 118–120
  challenges of, 17–18
  digital by default, 22–23
  disadvantages of, 94
  early case study, 18–20
  less effective for, 95
  transition to, 20–22
Virtual events team
  camera and sound operators,
    182–183
  event technologist, 180–181
  executive producer, 181–182
Vista Equity Partners, 192
VSef, 76

Warby Parker, 40, 44
Whalebone, 194

Wilson, Mark, 110
Wired magazine, 53
Working with Emotional Intelligence,
      160
Wow factor, 132–133

x.ai (artificial intelligence scheduling
      tool), 194

Zoom, 193
Zoom fatigue, 82